CONTINUUM CHARACTER STUDIES

TWELFTH NIGHT
CHARACTER STUDIES

GRAHAM ATKIN

continuum

Continuum
The Tower Building
11 York Road
London SE1 7NX

80 Maiden Lane, Suite 704
New York
NY 10038

www.continuumbooks.com

First published 2008

British Library Cataloguing-in-Publication Data
A catalogue record for this book is available from the British Library.

ISBN: 978-0-8264-9540-2 (hardback)
978-0-8264-9541-9 (paperback)

Library of Congress Cataloguing-in-Publication Data
A catalog record for this book is available from the Library of
Congress.

Typeset by Servis Filmsetting Ltd, Manchester
Printed and bound in Great Britain by
MPG Books Ltd, Bodmin, Cornwall

To B. J. Atkin

CONTENTS

ACKNOWLEDGEMENTS

I would like to thank all those who supported me while writing this book, in particular the series editor Ashley Chantler whose patience, attention to detail and good humour helped immensely.

SERIES EDITOR'S PREFACE

This series aims to promote sophisticated literary analysis through the concept of character. It demonstrates the necessity of linking character analysis to texts' themes, issues and ideas, and encourages students to embrace the complexity of literary characters and the texts in which they appear. The series thus fosters close critical reading and evidence-based discussion, as well as an engagement with historical context, and with literary criticism and theory.

Character Studies was prompted by a general concern in literature departments about students responding to literary characters as if they were real people rather than fictional creations, and writing about them as if they were two-dimensional entities existing in an ahistorical space. Some students tend to think it is enough to observe that King Lear goes 'mad', that Frankenstein is 'ambitious', or that Vladimir and Estragon are 'tender and cruel'. Their comments are correct, but obviously limited.

Thomas Docherty, in his *Reading (Absent) Character: Towards a Theory of Characterization in Fiction*, reminds us to relate characters to ideas but also stresses the necessity of engaging with the complexity of characters:

> If we proceed with the same theory as we apply to allegory [that a character represents one thing, such as Obstinate in Bunyan's *Pilgrim's Progress*], then we will be led to accept that Madame Bovary 'means' or 'represents' some one essence or value, however complex that essence may be. But perhaps, and more likely, she is many things, and perhaps some of them lead to her character being incoherent, lacking unity, and so

on. [. . .] It is clearly wrong to say, in a critical reading, that
Kurtz, for example, in Conrad's *Heart of Darkness* represents
evil, or ambition, or any other one thing, and to leave it at that;
nor is Jude a representative of 'failed aspirations' in Hardy's
Jude the Obscure; nor is Heathcliff a representation of the pro-
letariat in Emily Brontë's *Wuthering Heights*, and so on. There
may be elements of truth in some of these readings of character, but the theory which rests content with trying to discover the singular simple essence of character in this way is
inadequate [. . .] (1983, p. xii)

King Lear, for example, is complex, so not easily understandable,
and is perhaps 'incoherent, lacking unity'; he is fictional, so must
be treated as a construct; and he does not 'mean' or 'represent'
one thing. We can relate him to ideas about power, control,
judgement, value, sovereignty, the public and the private, sex and
sexuality, the body, nature and nurture, appearance, inheritance,
socialization, patriarchy, religion, will, blindness, sanity, violence, pessimism, hope, ageing, love, death, grief – and so on.

To ignore this, and to respond to Lear as if he is a real person
talking ahistorically, means we simplify both the character and
the play; it means, in short, that we forget our responsibilities as
literary critics. When, for example, Lear cries, 'Howl, howl, howl,
howl! O, you are men of stones!' (5.2.255), it would be wrong to
ignore our emotional response, to marginalize our empathy for a
father carrying his dead daughter, but we must also engage with
such other elements as: the meaning and repetition of 'Howl'
(three howls in some editions, four in others); the uncertainty
about to whom 'you are men of stones' is directed; what 'men of
stones' meant to Shakespeare's audience; the various ways in
which the line can be said, and the various effects produced; how
what Lear says relates to certain issues in the play and introduces
new ideas about being human; what literary critics have written
about the line; and what literary theorists have said, or might say,
about it.

When we embrace the complexity of character, when we
undertake detailed, sensitive critical analysis that acknowledges
historical context, and literary criticism and theory, and when we

relate characters to themes, issues and ideas, the texts we study blossom, beautifully and wonderfully, and we realize that we have so much more to say about them. We are also reminded of why they are worthy of study, of why they are important, of why they are great.

Ashley Chantler
University of Chester, UK

AN OVERVIEW OF *TWELFTH NIGHT*

Twelfth Night is a play ideally suited for the Character Studies series as it includes many memorable and engaging characters, such as Sir Toby Belch, Sir Andrew Aguecheek, Feste, Viola, Olivia, Orsino and Malvolio. The characters are interesting in themselves, but through an analysis centred on them it is possible to move into a myriad other areas, critical, thematic and theoretical, such as: the nature of comedy, festivity and the carnivalesque; the staging of desire and cruelty; the ever-changing nature of living language and witty wordplay; the representation of time and love.

AN OVERVIEW OF *TWELFTH NIGHT*

Twelfth Night is one of Shakespeare's most popular comedies. Probably written in 1601 and first performed in early 1602, the play centres on the mercurial figure of Viola, shipwrecked in Illyria and believing her identical twin brother Sebastian drowned. Viola makes a decision to disguise herself as a young man, Cesario, and to seek employment at the court of the lovesick Duke Orsino. When Orsino sends Cesario to woo Olivia, a local countess, on his behalf, Olivia falls in love with Viola/Cesario. It is in Olivia's household that we meet with other strong characters, such as her uncle Toby Belch and his hapless sidekick Sir Andrew Aguecheek. Malvolio, Olivia's steward, attempts to keep the riotous Belch in order, with limited success. Maria, Olivia's waiting-gentlewoman, Belch, Aguecheek, Feste and Fabian, fuelled by a sense of outrage at Malvolio's killjoy attitude, hatch a plot to humiliate the priggish steward. Feste, Olivia's jester, is a somewhat melancholic character who helps to weave the disparate parts of the plot together with his songs and punning wordplay. The treatment of Malvolio may begin as a practical joke, but ends in cruelty as he is imprisoned in the dark. When he is released at the play's end he vows revenge, striking a discordant note in what might be seen as the otherwise harmonious multiple-marriage resolution. Through the identical twin device Shakespeare manipulates the play into a concordant conclusion (notwithstanding Malvolio's bitterness, Antonio's disappointment – he seems thwarted in his desire for Sebastian – and Feste's odd mixture of vengefulness and aloofness) in which Sebastian and Viola are reunited and paired off with Olivia and Orsino respectively. It seems also that Maria and Toby will be married.

John Draper, in his study of the play and its characters in their Elizabethan context, *The Twelfth Night of Shakespeare's Audience*, suggests that 'the detailed episodes of this major plot arise naturally from the personalities and social planes of the characters concerned, and also grow reasonably from one another' (p. 216) and, concurring with this view, it seems fitting that we look carefully at the remarkable characters of this play as a healthy starting point for a rich engagement with *Twelfth Night*. This study will consider how the characters involved in this story are textually constructed by Shakespeare, but will also reflect on the play's performance history, with special attention paid to Trevor Nunn's acclaimed film version of 1996 (as this film is widely available it is more likely to provide a convenient reference to a particular rendering of the play that readers of this book may have access to than references to other, less known film versions, or to stage productions of which only a small number of readers may have knowledge). Though the book will situate *Twelfth Night* in relation to the conventions of early-modern dramatic comedy, particular attention will be paid to the 'darker' side of the comedy and critical preoccupation with the discordant and puzzling aspects of the play.

The characters of *Twelfth Night* are a motley crew who, through their amusing, and at times bitter, interplay combine to create the peculiar world of Shakespeare's Illyria. This study begins with a consideration of 'characters' on the early-modern stage and methods of characterization available to the playwright, before proceeding to a textual analysis of each of the main characters in the play, looking at how what they say and do, and what is said about them, creates the illusion of 'character'. The question of dramatic characterization will be discussed in relation to each figure. Each chapter will also contain a brief discussion of how performances of the play can stimulate thoughtfulness about the nature of Shakespeare's creation. The particular concentration in this regard will, as I say, be on the 1996 film version directed by Trevor Nunn, starring Ben Kingsley as Feste, Nigel Hawthorne as Malvolio and Imogen Stubbs as Viola.

AN OVERVIEW OF SHAKESPEARE'S COMEDY

Twelfth Night first appeared in print in the First Folio of Shakespeare's plays, published in 1623, seven years after the playwright's death in 1616. In this most remarkable of books there is a title page, or 'Catalogue of the severall Comedies, Histories, and Tragedies contained in this Volume', in which Shakespeare's plays are divided into Comedies, Histories and Tragedies, and the list of Comedies runs as follows (I have retained the spelling, capitalization and (minimal) punctuation from the First Folio Catalogue):

The Tempest
The two Gentlemen of Verona
The Merry Wives of Windsor
Measure for Measure
The Comedy of Errors
Much ado about Nothing
Loves Labour lost
Midsommer Nights Dreame
The Merchant of Venice
As you Like it
The Taming of the Shrew

All is well, that Ends well
Twelfe-Night, or what you will
The Winters Tale

It is a remarkable list of fourteen comedies (compared with ten
histories and eleven tragedies), not, it seems, listed in any particular order. Dates for the writing of these plays and their first performances are debated, but the list as given in the First Folio does
not give any indication in this respect. *Twelfth Night* appears with
its alternative title of 'what you will', and when we turn to page
255 and begin reading we are confronted with one of the most
famous of Shakespeare's play openings:

Enter Orsino Duke of Illyria, Curio, and other Lords.
Duke. IF Musicke be the food of Loue, play on,
Giue me excesse of it: that surfetting,
The appetite may sicken, and so dye.

It is a play that contains many ingredients in common with other
comedies by Shakespeare: disguise and mistaken identity; trick-
ery and wit with words; tricks of fate and circumstance; practical jokes; slapstick humour; music and dance; a celebration of
the regenerative powers of festivity; and somewhat miraculous or
contrived endings which feature, or look forward to, imminent
marriage(s). *Twelfth Night* also shares another, perhaps less
expected, ingredient with other comedies, and that is its melan-
cholia. Quite frankly, many of Shakespeare's so-called comedies
contain sad and serious subject matter which makes it difficult to
find them 'funny'. Throughout this book this question, concerning the essential nature of this popular play, will be discussed.
What kind of play is *Twelfth Night*? How should it be played?
How should it be interpreted? Is it a happy comedy, a dark
problem play, or an averted tragedy?

Most of Shakespeare's comedies were written in the first
decade of his career, in the 1590s, and after *Twelfth Night* he
perhaps wrote only four more comedies: *All's Well That Ends
Well*, *Measure for Measure*, *The Winter's Tale* and *The Tempest*.
But labelling these four plays comedies at all is problematic, for

they seem to resist such simple categorization. This means that we might see *Twelfth Night* as one of Shakespeare's late comedies, and if we consider what other plays Shakespeare had been writing or was soon to write it seems clear that it is not too surprising that this comedy should contain some darker and more sombre aspects than, say, the early comedy of *A Midsummer Night's Dream*. For *Twelfth Night* was probably written in around 1600–1, when Shakespeare would have also been working on *As You Like It* and *Hamlet*, and before his great outpouring of tragedies such as *Othello*, *King Lear*, *Macbeth* and *Antony and Cleopatra*.

STRUCTURE OF THE BOOK

In the first chapter, 'Shakespeare's Characters', an emphasis will be placed on considering the techniques of characterization available to Shakespeare and how he employs these techniques. There will also be a discussion of the use of the word 'character' and its development from a term referring to inscription to its more common current usage, as a term suggestive of personality.

Chapters 2 to 8 focus on the characters of the play in their order of appearance. In Chapters 2 and 3, Orsino and Viola are considered, and in Chapter 4 the grouping of Sir Toby Belch, Maria and Sir Andrew Aguecheek is discussed. Chapters 5, 6 and 7 focus on Feste (and Fabian), Olivia and Malvolio respectively. In Chapter 8, the characters of Antonio and Sebastian are analysed.

In the Conclusion, the emphasis is on moving beyond character into the key themes and issues of the play, some of which will have been raised in the earlier chapters. This final chapter is designed to provide readers with a thoughtful springboard for further enquiries into the play and its interpretation. The Conclusion is divided into three sections: 'Comedy and Carnival', 'Staging Desire and Cruelty' and 'Language and Time'. This final chapter is followed by suggestions for further reading, a full bibliography and an index to assist you in getting the most out of this book. The main aim here is to provide a book that will encourage thoughtful engagement with the text of Shakespeare's

Twelfth Night, in the first instance through consideration of its fascinating characters and, in turn, by inspiring an appetite for further investigation into, and rumination on, the play's cultural context, critical reception and performance history.

NOTE ON THE EDITION USED

Unless otherwise indicated, references to the play are taken from the Oxford World's Classics edition of *Twelfth Night*, edited by Roger Warren and Stanley Wells (Oxford: Oxford University Press, 1994). This edition is cited throughout as 'Warren'. Other editions of the play, and secondary works, used in the preparation of this book are given in the Guide to Further Reading and Bibliography at the end of this volume.

CHAPTER 1

SHAKESPEARE'S CHARACTERS

SHAKESPEARE AND 'CHARACTER'

In the second scene of the play, in which we first encounter Viola, she compliments the Sea-Captain who accompanies her thus:

> There is a fair behaviour in thee, captain,
> And though that nature with a beauteous wall
> Doth oft close in pollution, yet of thee
> I will believe thou hast a mind that suits
> With this thy fair and outward character. (1.2.44–8)

Viola's use of the word 'character' here is perhaps one of the earliest instances of the shift in meaning from the now antiquated sense of 'character' as inscription (marks or letters) to the more common modern sense of 'character' as denoting an individual person's particular qualities. In his sonnets Shakespeare memorably uses the term 'character' in its sense of a mark made with language to communicate faithfully that which is within: 'What's in the brain that ink may character / Which hath not figured to thee my true spirit?' (Sonnet 108). Viola suggests that though appearances are often deceptive, in the case of the Captain she will believe that he is as 'fair' as his 'outward' form suggests. Her awareness that one may appear to be other than what one really is spurs her on to ask the Captain to assist her to 'conceal me what I am' (1.2.50), and this decision to disguise herself sets the comedy in proper motion. She plans to present a 'character' to the world which is essentially false – her outward form and behaviour will denote 'male eunuch', but within she will remain a woman (though we cannot forget that on Shakespeare's stage she would have been played by a young man, which increases the sense of disjunction between outward character and inner reality). Her disguise will 'become / The form of my intent' (1.2.52); that is, as the Oxford editors note, 'be fitting for carrying out my purpose (literally, 'the shape of what I intend')' (p. 92). The multiple layers of concealment of 'character' in the modern sense of the true essence of an individual, beneath 'character' in the older sense of an outward inscription (clothing and behaviour that constitute a disguise or semblance), make Shakespeare's theatre an arena for complex and fascinating meditations on human identity and its relation to appearances. This is, of course, a preoccupation of Shakespeare, for whom, as we know, 'All the world's a stage' (*As You Like It*, 2.7.139).

The entire sonnet referred to above runs as follows:

> What's in the brain that ink may character
> Which hath not figured to thee my true spirit?
> What's new to speak, what now to register,
> That may express my love or thy dear merit?
> Nothing, sweet boy; but yet, like prayers divine,
> I must each day say o'er the very same,
> Counting no old thing old – thou mine, I thine –
> Even as when first I hallowed thy fair name.
> So that eternal love in love's fresh case
> Weighs not the dust and injury of age,
> Nor gives to necessary wrinkles place,
> But makes antiquity for aye his page,
> Finding the first conceit of love there bred
> Where time and outward form would show it dead. (Sonnet 108)

Here Shakespeare celebrates the eternally renewing power of love, a love not prone to ageing and decay, even though outward forms (the wrinkled and dying human animal) suggest otherwise. It is a love which Shakespeare aims to bring forth from his brain and 'character' in ink, so that he might 'figure', 'register', 'express' his true spirit. In *Twelfth Night* it is arguably in the character of Viola that this true spirit of love is most clearly and effectively figured, registered and expressed. It might seem fitting, therefore, for Shakespeare to open his play with Viola, shipwrecked on Illyria's shore. It is interesting to note that some interpreters of the play for performance, for example directors Kenneth Branagh and Trevor Nunn, do indeed make this decision to begin with Viola. However, Shakespeare chooses to open *Twelfth Night* with the brooding figure of Orsino, the Duke of Illyria, and it is with him that we begin our character analysis in the next chapter.

How is our impression of character formed? Playwrights can employ both explicit and implicit techniques of characterization when they put pen to paper. To begin with they can give characters telling or suggestive names, such as Toby Belch and Andrew Aguecheek (the former suggests rotundity and indigestion, presumably from a life of excessive drinking and eating; the latter suggests a pale, wan, rather sickly individual – 'ague' is fever). Viola, Olivia, Malvolio and Feste all have names which might be said to be significant in the interpretation of their characters and of the play they appear in (of which more in later chapters). The playwright could employ description in the stage directions, giving readers and performers clear guidance as to how to envisage or portray different characters. This is not something Shakespeare does, as he works through the speech of his characters, implying their behaviour in the words they speak or that others speak of them. The lack of lengthy prescriptive stage directions allows for an openness in the interpretation of Shakespeare's plays and their characters which readers, actors and directors find liberating.

Shakespeare certainly employs correspondence and contrast as a technique of characterization. Correspondence is employed most notably in this play with the use of identical twins, corresponding so closely to each other that even those who know them well cannot tell them apart. When Antonio sees Sebastian and Viola alongside each other he asks: 'How have you made division of yourself? / An apple cleft in two is not more twin / Than these two creatures. Which is Sebastian?' (5.1.216–18).

Contrast is employed with Sir Andrew Aguecheek and Sir Toby Belch, whose names imply that one is tall and thin-faced, the other plump and round-faced. They truly are an early-modern Laurel and Hardy. We can even think of correspondence between seemingly unlike characters. Orsino and Olivia, for example, share a tendency to self-indulgent excess. Viola and Feste (and to some extent Olivia) share an enjoyment of witty banter and wordplay. Olivia and Malvolio share an appearance of stuffiness which is dramatically reversed in the topsy-turvy madness of the play.

Confronted by the text alone we have the words assigned to each character – so a central key to the character must be what the character says. As well as forming an impression of a character from what they say, they may specifically make comments about themselves, whether in soliloquy or in dialogue with another. Our impression of an individual is also influenced by comments made by other characters. As people do, characters often talk about other characters; again, either in soliloquy or as part of dialogue (and either when the character talked about is present or absent). This commentary by others might also occur before, during or after the first appearance of a particular character. Characters might also be represented through their 'characters', that is, their letters, giving them a presence and a voice even when they are not actually on stage (if the letter is read aloud). Letters often feature in Shakespeare's drama, and *Twelfth Night* contains some notable examples: Maria's letter to Malvolio, which he takes to be Olivia's; Malvolio's letter to Olivia from his prison cell; and Sir Andrew's letter of challenge to Viola.

This short analysis of the ways a playwright develops character, explicitly through self-commentary or commentary by others, suggests the possibility of complex (and sometimes seemingly contradictory) effects achievable in the play-text. When we consider performance possibilities these complexities increase dramatically.

In performance all sorts of factors combine to form our impression of a character. These factors overwhelmingly derive from the actor's physical characteristics. First there are the qualities of voice. J. L. Styan has referred to these 'elements in the voice' as 'the five Ps' or 'the five Ss'. The five Ps are Pressure, Pace, Power, Pitch, Pause. The five Ss are Stress, Speed, Strength, Song, Silence (Styan 1965, pp. 38–9). These qualities in the voice require decisions from an actor and director, decisions which can have a significant impact on the effect of words which, to those who merely read the words on the page silently, are not settled. Other non-verbal decisions have to be made by those involved in performance. Some of these decisions are made at the stage of casting, as a particular actor is chosen over another, with different physical traits, stature and physiognomy. As an actor performs he or she, in consultation or not with their director, has to decide on facial expression, gestures and characteristic behaviour. Decisions also have to be made concerning mask and makeup, costume and properties ('props') that an actor may use in their performance. This is a benefit the reader has over the performer: the reader can consider many possible performances. The particular performer, at least in the precise moment of performance, must choose one interpretation (he or she could change this with each performance – but each individual performance will necessarily render a particular and singular interpretation).

Interestingly, with film and audio recording, these performances are reified – frozen – and can be looked at and heard again and again by the observer or listener, and commented on as fixed and lasting interpretations. It has been decided that, for this volume, where performance of the play is discussed, the main emphasis will be placed on Trevor Nunn's critically acclaimed 1996 film version – a rendering of the play that most readers of this book will have access to – and in which the casting of actors in the main roles leads to some interesting insights into character. Actors and directors are thoughtful interpreters of play-texts, often through the demands of performance, pushing their analyses further than academic critics. It is a welcome development in the study of plays, and Shakespeare in particular, that accounts of different stage and film performances have become more and more a part of the body of critical responses.

SHAKESPEARE'S STAGE

Though it is a blindingly obvious point to make it is nevertheless so fundamental as to be worth stressing at the outset that Shakespeare's *Twelfth Night* is a play that was written for performance, and written for performance in a theatre and a culture very different from our own. Some awareness of the stage and culture that Shakespeare wrote for is helpful to have in mind before we start to think about the characters of his play, and before we then move beyond character to key themes and issues.

The Globe Theatre was built on the south bank of the Thames in London in 1598–9, possibly from the remains of the first theatre to be built in London, by Richard Burbage in 1576. If you visit London today you can visit Shakespeare's Globe Theatre, for it has been rebuilt, near to where it originally stood, largely thanks to the drive and vision of the American actor Sam Wanamaker who, on visiting London, was surprised that no Globe Theatre could be found and decided to build a new one. Visiting the new Globe and seeing a play staged there is one of the best ways of imagining Shakespeare's original theatre. The original Globe Theatre unfortunately burnt down in 1613 and was rebuilt the following year. The second Globe was pulled down in 1644 'to make tenements in the room of it' (Halliday, 1964, p. 189).

Twelfth Night was most likely performed at the Globe Theatre in Shakespeare's day, but the only documented record of a performance before 1616, when Shakespeare died, is in the diary of John Manningham, who saw the play performed on 2 February 1602, at Middle Temple Hall, a centre of legal study in London (see Chapter Seven for a further discussion of Manningham's account of what he saw). Leslie Hotson argues that the play was first performed at Whitehall a year earlier than this, in 1601, and in his book *The First Night of Twelfth Night* (1954) he gathers circumstantial evidence to support his case.

Though we cannot, beyond Manningham's reference, be certain when and where *Twelfth Night* was performed in Shakespeare's London, we should be aware of essential differences between theatre now and then. The Elizabethans talked of hearing a play rather than seeing it, and the spoken words did far more of the work in terms of setting the scene than is generally the case in modern theatre. So with *Twelfth Night* we know we are in Illyria not because of an elaborate Illyrian set, but because Viola is told, in answer to her question 'What country, friends, is this?', 'This is Illyria, lady' (1.2.1). There were few lighting effects in Shakespeare's theatre, with performances traditionally taking place in the daylight. One major difference from today's theatre is that in Shakespeare's day there were no women acting on the stage. All parts were played by male actors. This fact about Shakespeare's stage must be remembered when thinking about *Twelfth Night*, for it had a considerable impact on the writing and performing of this play. Viola, Maria and Olivia were all originally played by males, and when Shakespeare wrote his play he knew he was writing these female parts for performance by male actors.

Of course, outside Shakespeare's Globe Theatre, the Middle Temple Hall and Whitehall there was a whole world that necessarily impinged on what went on within. London in the 1590s and early 1600s was a vibrant city whose people were hungry for entertainment. There will be more to be said about the Elizabethan context of Shakespeare's *Twelfth Night* in the Conclusion, but for now let us consider one cultural context that is nearly lost to us which has a particular importance when thinking about characters in Shakespeare's plays. This is the knowledge of the theory of the four humours, which would have been well known to Shakespeare and his audience. John Draper argues that the four humours theory is essential to Shakespeare's portrayal of character in *Twelfth Night* and he asserts that the humours' 'incongruity to a character's situation or social aspirations starts the plot in motion; their [the humours] well-known patterns guide the actions and reactions of various characters to these actions; and the outcome of this pattern supplies an inevitable end' (Draper 1950, p. 228). Certainly knowledge of the theory of the four humours (blood, phlegm, black bile and yellow bile) and the way that imbalances of these humours in the body were believed to relate to character (stated simply, an excess of blood makes one sanguine, too much phlegm makes one phlegmatic, excess of black bile makes one melancholic and too much yellow bile makes one choleric) are at work in Shakespeare's play (though perhaps Draper pushes his analysis too far for the tastes of modern readers). Though knowledge of the humours is helpful if we want to make sense of the many references in Shakespeare's plays to them, nevertheless it is part of Shakespeare's supreme achievement that he moves beyond such classical and medieval ideas to present characters on his stage who are complex and often inconsistent in their actions. One of his great inspirations is the French philosopher and writer Michel de Montaigne who, it is thought, had a significant influence on Shakespeare's thinking about character and the self. The following quotation from Montaigne's essay 'On the Inconstancy of Our Actions' is indicative:

> We are entirely made up of bits and pieces, woven together so diversely and so shapelessly that each one of them pulls its own way at every moment. And there is as much difference between us and ourselves as there is between us and other people. (Montaigne 1987, p. 380)

Again and again Shakespeare's characters give voice to Montaigne's sense of the essential impermanence and changeability of the self, and in *Twelfth Night* we find this most memorably expressed in Viola's 'I am not what I am' (3.1.139).

SHAKESPEARE'S ACTORS

When thinking about characters in Shakespeare's plays some consideration ought to be given to the actors for whom Shakespeare wrote, including himself. There is no incontrovertible evidence, but it is conjectured by some that Shakespeare may have played the part of Malvolio (Ackroyd 2005, p. 384). The part of Feste the clown is widely thought to have been written by Shakespeare with the particular comic actor and musician Robert Armin in mind. This same multi-talented performer probably played Touchstone in *As You Like It* and also the fool in *King Lear* (Goldsmith 1974, p. 51). But who played Viola, or Orsino, or Sir Toby Belch? Firm evidence is lacking, but we do possess, from the First Folio, a list of 'The Names of the Principall Actors in all these Playes' which includes the names of Robert Armin, William Kempe, John Hemmings, Richard Burbage and Henry Condell. Even if they have no direct experience of the processes of putting on plays, students of Shakespeare should be encouraged to maintain a thoughtfulness about the collaborative nature of theatre. As Jonathan Bate points out in his impressive but accessible new edition of Shakespeare's *Complete Works* (based on the First Folio): 'Public playhouses and professional full-time acting companies reliant on the market for their income were born in Shakespeare's childhood. When he arrived in London as a man, a new phenomenon was in the making: the actor who is so successful that he becomes a "star"' (Bate and Rasmussen 2007, p. 13). The First Folio itself, we should remember, was compiled by two of Shakespeare's fellow actors, John Hemmings and Henry Condell.

As well as thinking about Shakespeare's original actors we might also think about all the other actors who have interpreted these characters and performed these parts. Certainly for the actor rehearsing a part for performance the idea that the character is not real is at best unhelpful and at worst impossible. The task facing the actor preparing to perform the part of Sir Toby, or Viola, or Feste is, arguably, the task of finding the character, of making the character make sense, of bringing the character to life. It is a task that is very different from the literary critic's approach (though more and more in Shakespeare studies there is an emphasis on the myriad aspects of performance). As Paul Edmondson writes in his extremely helpful handbook on *Twelfth Night*:

> Today's criticism tends to eschew any notion of identifiable 'characters' and sees Shakespeare's roles as politically and historically inscribed textual constructs. However, some modern criticism does still continue to read for character and this practice is certainly alive and well in the teaching of Shakespeare in secondary schools. This interpretative and critical act can be enlivened and refreshed by a consideration

of performance. After all, actors are continually practising character criticism. (Edmondson 2005, p. 70)

This book falls into the bracket of 'some modern criticism' mentioned by Edmondson that 'does still continue to read for character' and its author wholly endorses the consideration of performance as a means of enlivening and refreshing your own interpretations and criticisms of the characters and the plays that you read and study. Some of the most interesting insights into plays are provided by actors who necessarily reflect deeply on their character and on that character's relation to the other characters in the play. The process of rehearsal with other actors and a director constitutes a series of interpretative critical acts and experiments to bring the text into being as performance.

It has often been observed that an essential of effective drama is conflict of some sort, whether within or between characters. As Draper suggests: 'drama requires an initial instability [. . .] high comedy, based on character, demands that this inequilibrium be fundamentally apparent in the major personalities' (Draper 1950, pp. 226–7). And this is the case in *Twelfth Night* in which, in keeping with Draper's analysis of true comedy, 'the plot [. . .] must grow out of the chief characters' (p. 97). This is a challenge to Aristotle's identification and ordering of the constituent parts of tragedy in his *Poetics*. Aristotle identifies six constituents of tragedy and lists them in order of importance. They are: Plot, Character, Thought, Diction, Spectacle and Song. Though he is writing about tragedy he does say that 'all plays alike possess' these constituents (Aristotle 1965, p. 39). Shakespeare's characterization in *Twelfth Night* is 'within itself consistent even in the most complex personalities; and, furthermore, it is perfectly integrated with the plot and with the comic effects of the dialogue' (Draper 1950, p. 230). To be sure, as Draper claims, 'if the number of complex characters be any index of a comedy's excellence, *Twelfth Night* deserves to rank among the greatest ever penned; for Shakespeare has bestowed this crowning reality of life on no less than five of its characters [Sir Toby, Maria, Malvolio, Feste and Olivia]' (p. 225). Draper's estimate could be considered conservative, even parsimonious. Viola, it seems, should be added to this list, and perhaps Sir Andrew, Orsino and the passionate Antonio.

MUSIC, SONG AND DANCE

Twelfth Night is a play that begins with music and ends in song. It also contains a fair amount of mad cavorting and dance, particularly from Andrew Aguecheek and Toby Belch. When we first meet this pair in Act 1 Scene 3 we witness Sir Andrew capering in an absurd manner as Sir Toby eggs him on: 'let me see thee caper / Ha, higher!' (1.3.131–2). Various forms of dance are mentioned here, for example the 'galliard', 'the back-trick', 'a coranto', 'a jig', 'a cinquepace' (1.3.112–25), and we imagine that as Andrew sets 'about some revels' (1.3.127) he incorporates a number, perhaps all, of them in his antics. A good critical edition, such as the Oxford World's Classics edition used here, gives us helpful information on such matters. We read that a 'galliard' is 'a lively dance of five steps, the fifth a caper'; a 'caper' is a 'leap', though it allows Toby a pun 'on the sense "pickled flower-buds, used for sauce to season mutton" '; 'the back-trick' is 'a vigorous kick of the foot behind the body'; a 'coranto' is 'a running dance', 'even faster than a galliard'; and finally that a 'cinquepace', from the French for 'five steps', 'was equivalent to a galliard' (Warren, p. 99). This variety of movements demonstrated by Sir Andrew for the amusement of Sir Toby provides the actor playing Aguecheek with the opportunity to entertain the audience with some virtuoso physical comedy. In Trevor Nunn's film Sir Andrew's part is played by Richard E. Grant, whose capering galliard, while Mel Smith's Sir Toby accompanies him on the piano, provides a magnificently humorous combination of lively music and absurd comic dancing that does more to set the tone of festive revelry than anything the characters might say.

In the riotous drunken excesses of Act 2 Scene 3 Feste sings 'a love-song' before Aguecheek, and Belch and Feste sing the catch 'hold thy peace, thou knave' (a catch is a song in which 'the singers start one after another, repeating the song vigorously and boisterously' (Warren, p. 126)). Sir Toby then mentions other songs, possibly singing parts of them ('Peg-o-Ramsey' and 'Three merry men be we' and 'There dwelt a man in Babylon, lady, lady'), before he finally settles on 'O' the twelfth day of December' (2.3.72–9). Shakespeare here creates a sense of hubbub and chaos which the disapproving Malvolio attempts to quell, unsuccessfully trying as he does to assert some sense of respect for the peace of Olivia's household. When we read this scene we must imagine the noise and manic behaviour of the drunken revellers, and Malvolio's not-unreasonable requests for an end to the disorder. Without a keen imaginative sense of performance the humour and tension of the scene will be lost on the play-text reader.

Let us end this chapter with a passionate passage from one of the most enthusiastic critics of *Twelfth Night*, John Draper, who understands well the depth of meaning in the world of Illyria and its characters. His vehemence and energy is contagious:

> Our ignorance of Elizabethan social life has obscured his realism; our ignorance of the theory of humors in its psychological ramifications has obscured the subtle unity and depth of his characterisation; and only by relearning these backgrounds as the Elizabethans knew them can we interpret the plays as the Elizabethans saw them. Of course, no fine art can completely reproduce the intricacies of real life, but drama expresses more of its simultaneous facets than any other aesthetic medium; and Shakespeare's dramas express these intricate relations of man to man and man to his environment more fully and more vividly than the works of any other dramatist. This is the supreme virtue of his plays, and the very core of his subtle insight, and to gainsay this quality is to gainsay his highest excellence. He saw life steadily, and also saw it whole. (Draper 1950, pp. 231–2)

CHAPTER 2

ORSINO

John Draper's judgement of the Duke of Illyria seems essentially correct: he 'is the wellborn lover, a disappointed Romeo, elegant and charming but beclouded with melancholy' (1950, pp. 223–4). It is an impression of this character which quickly establishes itself in our minds, and never really changes. The one constant thing about Orsino is his brooding self-centredness. The play opens with Orsino's famous speech, a speech which does so much to set the mood and tone of the play and which introduces many of the recurring themes. It is a speech which also does much to form his character in our minds:

> If music be the food of love, play on,
> Give me excess of it, that surfeiting,
> The appetite may sicken and so die.
> That strain again, it had a dying fall.
> O, it came o'er my ear like the sweet sound
> That breathes upon a bank of violets,
> Stealing and giving odour. Enough, no more,
> 'Tis not so sweet now as it was before. (1.1.1–8)

We begin, then, with music that Orsino demands ('Give me') in abundance, a sad, sweet kind of music with a 'dying fall' suggestive of the languishing mood of the Duke, who suddenly and peevishly orders a cessation of such harmony with a bad-tempered and petulant 'Enough, no more', claiming that the music is no longer as 'sweet' as it was. We imagine the music is just as sweet; it is

Orsino whose perception of the music has altered. Our first impression of the Duke is of a rather fickle and self-indulgent ego-tistical man, and this impression is reinforced at the close of the first scene when we hear him praising Olivia's devotion to her dead brother and fantasizing about replacing him in her affections:

> O, she that hath a heart of that fine frame
> To pay this debt of love but to a brother,
> How will she love when the rich golden shaft
> Hath killed the flock of all affections else
> That live in her – when liver, brain, and heart,
> These sovereign thrones, are all supplied, and filled
> Her sweet perfections with one self king!
> Away before me to sweet beds of flowers:
> Love-thoughts lie rich when canopied with bowers. (1.1.32–40)

Again there is a sense of a man wallowing in his own emotions ('O, she'), more concerned with his own excellence ('supplied, and filled' 'with one self king') than the 'perfections' of Olivia. There is something a little clichéd about Orsino's final couplet here which suggests that Shakespeare wants to situate Orsino in our minds as a type of courtly lover, in love with the very idea of being in love and poetically reflecting on the torments that this unre-quited love brings. His language throughout this scene employs the conventional references to hearts, love and flowers of Petrarchan love sonnets, addressed to the idealized and unachiev-able female lover. Orsino has earlier deliberately mistaken Curio's invitation to hunt the hart, a stag, as a reference to his own heart, by replying in terms that focus attention on his own pained state, even going so far as to cast himself as Actaeon to Olivia's Diana:

> Curio: Will you go hunt, my lord?
> Orsino: What, Curio?
> Curio: The hart.
> Orsino: Why so I do, the noblest that I have.
> O, when mine eyes did see Olivia first
> Methought she purged the air of pestilence;
> That instant was I turned into a hart,

And my desires, like fell and cruel hounds,
E'er since pursue me. (1.1.16–22)

The allusion to Actaeon is important as it 'is a vivid way of expressing the ferocity of Orsino's frustrated desire for Olivia' (Warren, p. 87). The classical legend, told by Ovid in *Metamorphoses*, is of Actaeon the huntsman, who sees the virgin huntress goddess Diana naked. She punishes him by turning him into a stag. The story tells how his own hounds then pursue and savagely devour him. The reference by Orsino here to the legend of Actaeon and Diana, a story familiar to Shakespeare's Elizabethan audience, economically communicates a sense of his self-obsession. The heart/hart that he will hunt is his own. His description of his own desires pursuing his own heart 'like fell and cruel hounds' presents a hugely egotistical figure who sees himself as both hunter and hunted, lover and beloved. Orsino's love for Olivia has little to do with her in any real sense but only in the unachievable love-object she represents for him. She is as distant as a deity who, in a reference to the frequent threat of the plague which Elizabethans thought was caused by polluted air, even has the divine power to purge that air of 'pestilence'. (This reference to the plague is later echoed by Olivia, who refers to the suddenness with which she falls in love with Viola: 'even so quickly may one catch the plague' (1.5.250), suggesting her human vulnerability both to love and death rather than her immortal and chaste divinity.)

Our sense of Orsino's changeable nature is added to even before we next see him when Scene Four of the play opens with an exchange between Valentine, one of Orsino's appropriately named attendants, and Viola, now disguised as the eunuch Cesario:

Valentine: If the Duke continue these favours towards you, Cesario, you are like to be much advanced. He hath known you but three days, and already you are no stranger.
Viola: You either fear his humour or my negligence, that you call in question the continuance of his love. Is he inconstant, sir, in his favours?
Valentine: No, believe me. (1.4.1–8)

Valentine's defence of his master rings hollow here. It seems Viola has hit the nail on the head concerning Orsino's predominant characteristic, namely his fickle inconstancy. Valentine is perhaps a little put out by his master's 'favours' toward this fresh-faced newcomer.

Orsino seems to lack moderation; he is a figure of excessive emotion. He has, within three days, become so trusting of the 'good youth' (1.4.15) Cesario that he is able to declare to him/her: 'Thou know'st no less but all: I have unclasped / To thee the book even of my secret soul' (1.4.13–14). In contradiction of this clear indication of his pleasure in being with this 'dear lad' (1.4.29), whom he significantly compares to Diana, whose lip, he claims, 'is not more smooth and rubious' (1.4.32), there follows another suggestion of Orsino's changeable nature as he declares: 'I myself am best / When least in company' (1.4.37–8).

In the following scene, though physically absent, Orsino has a marginal presence through his text, which Viola has taken pains to learn in order to woo Olivia for her new master. He is also described by Olivia in a rather detached manner:

> Your lord does know my mind, I cannot love him.
> Yet I suppose him virtuous, know him noble,
> Of great estate, of fresh and stainless youth,
> In voices well divulged, free, learn'd, and valiant,
> And in the dimension and the shape of nature
> A gracious person; but yet I cannot love him.
> He might have took his answer long ago. (1.5.246–52)

Leslie Hotson argues for a reading of Orsino and his language which is at odds with most critical responses (and with the reading generally presented here). He claims that it is 'common form for critics to take turns dipping into the youthful and noble Orsino's dramatic character and coming up with the same thing: "sentimental and fancy-sick", "voluptuous love-languors", "a thistle-down amorist", "amorous and sentimental"'(1954, p. 124). This, Hotson argues, is a misreading, for Orsino's 'extreme sentiments take their proper place as excellent passages of Elizabethan poetic tribute, of "writing the Queen anew"' (p. 125). Hotson links Orsino's poetic mode of praise to similarly ecstatic effusions from Ralegh and Essex, two of Elizabeth's favourites. If Olivia is a 'shadow of the Queen' then Orsino '*must* court her, however hopelessly, and in terms of adoration too, until she chooses a husband' (p. 126). He is simply playing the game of the Elizabethan court and praising the Queen through the convention of being in love with her. There will be more representation and engagement with Hotson's ingenious historicized analysis of the play and its characters in subsequent chapters. Suffice to say for now that Hotson's view of Orsino's rhetoric is coherent, that it is based on thorough textual engagement and contextual research, and that it is stimulating for any reader of *Twelfth Night* to reflect on.

When Orsino later lectures Viola on love we must feel that he is given words to speak that will, in the light of his later transference of desire from Olivia to Viola, make his character appear ludicrous:

Come hither, boy. If ever thou shalt love,
In the sweet pangs of it remember me;
For such as I am, all true lovers are,
Unstaid and skittish in all motions else
Save in the constant image of the creature
That is beloved. (2.4.14–19)

The fact is that Orsino shows himself to be just as 'unstaid and skittish' in matters of love as in 'all motions else'. The textual evidence is clear for, in this same scene, within a few lines he is lecturing Cesario on the essential difference between men and women and claiming that 'however we do praise ourselves, / Our fancies are more giddy and unfirm, / More longing, wavering, sooner lost and worn, / Than women's are' (2.4.31–4). Orsino then veers back to his former position after Feste's exit.

A large part of the attraction Orsino feels for Viola is due to her impressive, sensitive and intelligent use of language. When we hear them, through the combination of their utterances, make 'a poignant statement of the price of perception' (Warren, p. 136) we sense a developing communion:

Orsino: Then let thy love be younger than thyself,
Or thy affection cannot hold the bent;
For women are as roses, whose fair flower
Being once displayed, doth fall that very hour.
Viola: And so they are. Alas that they are so:
To die even when they to perfection grow. (2.4.35–40)

It is as though Viola continues Orsino's melancholy thought; indeed it seems she develops his thought and gives it more of an erotic association with her play on 'die' (a common Elizabethan shorthand for orgasm) and her use of the word 'perfection', which can have, in this context, a kind of sexual significance of completion and consummation. Though the scene presents us with a woman disguised as a man discussing women (with a certain amount of sexual innuendo involved) with a man she is falling in love with, the fact that Shakespeare wrote the part for a young man to play must be remembered. Lisa Jardine, in her influential work *Still Harping on Daughters: Women and Drama in the Age of Shakespeare*, reminds us that 'the dependent role of the boy player doubles for the dependency which is woman's lot, creating a sensuality which is independent of the sex of the desired figure and which is particularly erotic where the sex is confused (when boy player represents woman, disguised as a dependent boy)' (1989, p. 24). The scene between Orsino and Viola quoted above presented Elizabethan audiences with a complex and sexually ambiguous situation which invited them into the erotic game-play between the Duke and his androgynous servant.

In spite of Hotson's argument, Orsino does strike us as a sentimental man, and he values Feste's singing as it evidently impresses, even moves him. Orsino seems genuinely glad to see Feste and invites him to sing, having made some remarks to Viola that denote the Illyrian Duke as one who fancies he appreciates and knows something of the origins and traditions of music and song:

O fellow, come, the song we had last night.
Mark it Cesario, it is old and plain.

The spinsters and the knitters in the sun,
And the free maids that weave their thread with bones,
Do use to chant it. It is silly sooth,
And dallies with the innocence of love,
Like the old age. (2.4.41–7)

Orsino's description of the song that Feste is to sing (for a further discussion of this song see Chapter Five) does not seem particularly accurate. Can it really be said to be 'silly sooth' and dallying 'with the innocence of love / Like the old age'? His assessment of the song seems to tell us more about himself than the song. The speech adds to our sense of Orsino as somehow removed from the action of the rest of the play, isolated from the world of festive frenzy, content in his own world of fancy, imagination, music, song and the escapism of the pastoral mode with its nostalgic retreat into an innocent and idealized golden age.

Feste the clown later tells Orsino straight to his face what we have been suspecting. His speech is a mixture of plain-speaking and riddling references:

Now the melancholy god protect thee, and the tailor make thy doublet of changeable taffeta, for thy mind is a very opal. I would have men of such constancy put to sea, that their business might be everything, and their intent everywhere, for that's it that always makes a good voyage of nothing. Farewell. (2.4.72–7)

The reference to 'changeable taffeta' is to 'silk whose colour changes with the light and angle of view', while 'thy mind is a very opal' refers to 'an iridescent gemstone' which makes it 'an image of changeability and inconstancy' (Warren, p. 138). Feste's point is clear here as he hits the Duke's character with a verbal bullseye.

As if to confirm Orsino's foolish pride in the intensity of his own feelings, and his incorrect sense of the permanence and strength of his love for Olivia, he declares, only a few lines following Feste's judgement of him, that:

> There is no woman's sides
> Can bide the beating of so strong a passion
> As love doth give my heart; no woman's heart
> So big, to hold so much. They lack retention.
> Alas, their love may be called appetite,
> No motion of the liver, but the palate,
> That suffer surfeit, cloyment, and revolt.
> But mine is all as hungry as the sea,
> And can digest as much. Make no compare
> Between that love a woman can bear me
> And that I owe Olivia. (2.4.92–102)

As the Oxford editors point out, 'Orsino criticizes women for indulging appetite to the point of *cloyment* (satiety) and *revolt* (revulsion, sickening), which is exactly what he wanted the music to do for him in the opening speech of the play' (Warren, p. 139). That we see him clearly fail to live up to his own grand claims of the retentive nature of his love for Olivia makes Orsino fool enough, but he is made more ridiculous by the fact that he speaks to the disguised Viola, who cannot keep silent and contradicts him with a heartfelt, 'Ay, but I know' (2.4.103), before going on to describe cryptically the depth of her own love for Orsino, a love presented as far more constant than his for Olivia.

When we see Orsino again it is the final scene of the play, and Feste manages, through his wit, to beg more money from him. On seeing Antonio, whom he recognizes, Orsino displays a side of his character hitherto unseen in the play, and he delivers a speech about Antonio's heroic martial deeds that also shows his own battle experience. It is a brief glimpse of Orsino as commanding, martial and regal:

> That face of his I do remember well,
> Yet when I saw it last it was besmeared
> As black as Vulcan in the smoke of war.
> A baubling vessel was he captain of,
> For shallow draught and bulk unprizable,
> With which such scatheful grapple did he make
> With the most noble bottom of our fleet

That very envy and the tongue of loss
Cried fame and honour on him. What's the matter? (5.1.45–53)

The speech powerfully creates in our minds images of Orsino
and Antonio as rivals in sea-battle, with 'the smoke of war'
surrounding them. Orsino shows himself capable of a noble generosity in his tribute to Antonio's valour. He also rather impres-
sively, and somewhat uncharacteristically given his behaviour
and demeanour in earlier scenes, takes command of the situation, accurately identifying Antonio and then demanding of his
first officer more information. This is a new decisive and active
Orsino to contrast with his earlier passivity. It reminds us that
Orsino is a Duke, a man who is used to commanding others and
being obeyed. Now that the play is nearing its close, it is significant that this side of Orsino's character should come to the fore,
for the temporary suspension of hierarchical difference is coming
to an end, and the aristocratic figures are assuming their traditionally dominant roles.

Then again it is the same old inconstant Orsino, who tires of
one tune and desires another, who can be said to be reflected in
his attitude to Olivia once Cesario is revealed as Viola. Orsino
does not for a moment bemoan the loss of his Countess, whose
entry in this final scene he has described hyperbolically: 'now
heaven walks on earth' (5.1.92). This excessive rhetoric is contin-
ued as he complains to the still disinterested (in him) Olivia: 'You
uncivil lady, / To whose ingrate and unauspicious altars / My soul
the faithfull'st off'rings hath breathed out / That e'er devotion
tendered – what shall I do?' (5.1.108–11). What he shall do is recognize that his interest lies elsewhere and that, by taking Viola as
his wife and leaving Olivia to Sebastian, he 'shall have share in
this most happy wreck' (5.1.260).

Orsino's petulance veers close to cruelty towards the play's
end when, thinking that Cesario has betrayed him by marrying
Olivia, he starkly threatens to do him physical harm, perhaps
even to kill him: 'Come, boy, with me, my thoughts are ripe in
mischief. / I'll sacrifice the lamb that I do love / To spite a raven's
heart within a dove' (5.1.125–7). He has already, it seems,
threatened Olivia, in a bad-tempered outburst in which he

presents his passion as a form of nobility that is hard to find convincing: 'Why should I not, had I the heart to do it, / Like to th' Egyptian thief at point of death, / Kill what I love – a savage jealousy / That sometime savours nobly' (5.1.113–16). What these quotations draw our attention to is the dangerous side of Orsino's character. He is a man who is used to getting what he wants and being thwarted makes him tetchy and potentially cruel. The movement of the play forbids Orsino's cruelty to be realized; however, it should be noted that Shakespeare has laced the slightly absurd melancholy of his Duke with a sense of threat. This threat of cruelty from Orsino raises issues of authority and power in the play. We must not forget that Orsino is an aristocratic figure whose self-indulgent behaviour is allowed because of his ruling-class status. Malvolio, for example, who displays similarly narcissistic traits to Orsino, is humiliated and ridiculed for having ideas above his station. Elliot Krieger, in his book *A Marxist Study of Shakespeare's Comedies*, highlights these issues of class in the play and convincingly argues that Orsino, as an aristocratic protagonist, is permitted a retreat from the community of the play and that furthermore, by 'withdrawing from the world, he has increased his power to control, or to feel in control of, the world' (1979, p. 105). Krieger's analysis of the play will be discussed further in subsequent chapters.

Directors of the play see Orsino's role as vital in setting the tone. John Caird argues that Orsino is a 'difficult, very ambiguous part to play, because you've got to be very strong and authoritative, yet you are in a sense the butt of a very big joke' (Billington 1990, p. 73), and John Barton concurs, pointing out that if Orsino is not played with sufficient weight 'he just becomes wet, and that trivialises Viola's feelings and the whole chemistry of the evening is affected' (p. 74). These insights, from those who have worked closely with the text to bring it alive in performance, are helpful to the reader in reminding us of the varying possibilities inherent in the text and, in the case of Orsino, of the changeable nature of the opal-minded Duke (see p. 25).

After his scene with Viola in Act 2 Scene 4 we do not see Orsino again until the final scene. In that scene in Act 2 his interest is seen to shift from Olivia to Viola in a series of questions: 'what dost thou know?' (2.4.104), 'and what's her history?' (2.4.109) and 'but died thy sister of her love, my boy?' (2.4.119). Much depends on how an actor says these lines (they could be spoken angrily and patronizingly, for example, or searchingly and tenderly). The scene offers an opportunity to suggest a strong attraction between Orsino and Viola, and the potentially hetero- and homoerotic charge of such an exchange can be brought out in performance. The sexually-charged play of the carnival atmosphere may crackle here, but by the play's end there is a reassertion of heterosexual patriarchy after the festive suspension of normal relations. Orsino's speech, first to Olivia, who has generously offered to have the weddings 'here at my house and at my proper cost' (5.1.310), and then to Viola, is a good example of his new poise:

> Madam, I am most apt t'embrace your offer.
> [*To Viola*] Your master quits you, and for your service done him
> So much against the mettle of your sex,
> So far beneath your soft and tender breeding,
> And since you called me master for so long,
> Here is my hand, you shall from this time be
> Your master's mistress. (5.1.311–17)

After the madness and confusion of the cross-dressing and gender-bending we have, at the play's end, the character of Orsino giving orders, sending someone (Fabian usually goes) out after Malvolio:

> Pursue him, and entreat him to a peace.
> He hath not told us of the captain yet. [*Exit Fabian*]
> When that is known, and golden time convents,
> A solemn combination shall be made
> Of our dear souls. Meantime, sweet sister,
> We will not part from hence. Cesario, come –
> For so you shall be while you are a man;
> But when in other habits you are seen,
> Orsino's mistress, and his fancy's queen. (5.1.370–8)

This is, to be sure, a problematic speech. Orsino seems to want proof that Viola is who she says she is. He also knows that she's a she, but will continue to address her as 'Cesario'. The term 'fancy's queen' is perhaps the strangest of the speech, for with this Orsino peculiarly places Viola as the embodiment of his desire, robbing her of any sense of autonomy while asserting the dominance of his own imagination.

Orsino commands someone to pursue Malvolio, partly to 'entreat him to a peace' (5.1.370), but also to learn of the whereabouts of the sea-captain whom Malvolio has himself imprisoned – for the captain has Viola's 'maid's garments' (5.1.269). Orsino declares that when these 'other habits' (5.1.377) are found, and Viola is seen in them, she can then be 'Orsino's mistress, and his fancy's queen' (5.1.378). Until then Orsino seems happy to prolong the homoerotic thrill and refers to his future wife as 'Cesario, come – / For so you shall be while you are a man' (5.1.375–6). Let us not forget that Orsino is a visitor in Olivia's house, but he does not hesitate to take command, addressing Olivia as 'sweet sister' (5.1.374) and informing her that 'we will not part from hence' (5.1.375) until the whereabouts of the sea-captain (and Viola's clothes) 'is known, and golden time convents, / A solemn combination shall be made / Of our dear souls' (5.1.372–4). This imperious and impressive speech strongly conveys a sense of ordered closure. However, in a final twist Shakespeare does not allow the Duke a complete reassertion of male power, as the play ends with Feste's enigmatic song, a song which undercuts the sense of closure and stability and leaves us instead feeling, perhaps like Feste, haunted by feelings of incompleteness and difficulty.

CHAPTER 3

VIOLA

CROSS-DRESSING VENUS

Viola is washed up on the shores of Illyria, like Venus created from the foam of the ocean. Botticelli's famous image of Venus hovering majestically toward the shore on her open shell, the dishiest goddess of them all, is well known, but worth pondering in relation to Viola in Shakespeare's play. Shakespeare is writing out of and for a culture steeped in interest in Greek and Roman myths. The echoes of Ovid's Venus washed up on the shore from the salt water would be understood by Shakespeare's audiences. Indeed, Viola's later line recalls the legend of Venus's birth, springing from the spilled seed of Jove on the water: 'Tempests are kind, and salt waves fresh in love!' (3.4.375). Like Botticelli's Venus, Shakespeare's Viola conceals herself, though the concealment, if anything, makes her more desirable. Certainly she quickly wins her way into Orsino's heart, and he is the character in Illyria with the highest status. The play ends with him referring to Viola as his 'fancy's queen', tying in neatly with the imaginative dominance of love in the Duke's mind. Along the way Viola also draws Olivia out of mourning for a dead brother and into the madness of love. Viola, as a kind of cross-dressing Venus, compels the self-indulgent Orsino and Olivia to look outside themselves, becoming Olivia's 'one self king' (1.1.38) and Orsino's 'fancy's queen' (5.1.378).

Viola's opening exchange with the loyal Captain conjures, with Shakespeare's characteristic brilliance of economy, a vivid scene:

> Viola: What country, friends, is this?
> Captain: This is Illyria, lady.
> Viola: And what should I do in Illyria?
> My brother he is in Elysium.
> Perchance he is not drowned. What think you sailors?
> Captain: It is perchance that you yourself were saved.
> Viola: O my poor brother! And so perchance may he be.
> (1.2.1–6)

Viola's brother is dead, she believes, but we learn this only after two questions which quickly establish this young woman as courteous and amiable ('friends') and forward-looking ('what should I do'). Illyria may be a place of love, but it is also a place of death, with its echoes of Elysium, the heavenly fields of classical mythology. Viola's mention of Elysium shows a hopefulness even in the face of disaster, for Elysium is a place of paradise. And Viola supplements the faith in her brother's immortality with the hope that he may not be drowned at all, finding comfort in the good fortune of her own survival. Thus it is that Shakespeare skilfully establishes Viola's characteristic optimism. In adversity she maintains a sweetness of disposition which embodies the spirit of love. Our first impression of Viola reminds us of what Orsino said in the play's opening scene: 'O spirit of love, how quick and fresh art thou' (1.1.9). Viola is quick-witted and fresh-faced and she is not only loved, but loves with an intense constancy unmatched by any other character in the play. Her appeal to the Captain to help her disguise herself as a young man informs us of some of her skills and abilities (for example, she can sing and is musical) but also presents a character who surrenders to time, not with any sense of fatalism, but with a positive energy that recognizes that some things are beyond her control while maintaining a confidence that her 'wit' will help her to realize her purpose ('the form of my intent'):

> I pray thee – and I'll pay thee bounteously –
> Conceal me what I am, and be my aid
> For such disguise as haply shall become
> The form of my intent. I'll serve this duke.

Thou shalt present me as an eunuch to him.
It may be worth thy pains, for I can sing,
And speak to him in many sorts of music
That will allow me very worth his service.
What else may hap, to time I will commit,
Only shape thou thy silence to my wit. (1.2.49–58)

We learn of Viola's love for Orsino in an aside: 'Yet a barful strife, / Whoe'er I woo, myself would be his wife' (1.4.41–2) and this begins a direct source of information for the audience which is further developed in her significant soliloquy, delivered after Malvolio has tried to give her the ring from Olivia:

I left no ring with her. What means this lady?
Fortune forbid my outside have not charmed her.
She made good view of me, indeed so much
That straight methought her eyes had lost her tongue,
For she did speak in starts, distractedly.
She loves me sure, the cunning of her passion
Invites me in this churlish messenger.
None of my lord's ring! Why, he sent her none.
I am the man. If it be so – as 'tis –
Poor lady, she were better love a dream!
Disguise, I see thou art a wickedness
Wherein the pregnant enemy does much.
How easy is it for the proper false
In women's waxen hearts to set their forms!
Alas, our frailty is the cause, not we,
For such as we are made of, such we be.
How will this fadge? My master loves her dearly,
And I, poor monster, fond as much on him,
And she, mistaken, seems to dote on me.
What will become of this? As I am man,
My state is desperate for my master's love.
As I am woman, now alas the day,
What thriftless sighs shall poor Olivia breathe!
O time, thou must untangle this, not I.
It is too hard a knot for me t'untie. (2.2.17–41)

Here Viola displays a thoughtfulness and perceptiveness that we cannot fail to admire. Her observation that Olivia 'loves me sure' is in no way arrogance, but demonstrates an understanding of the madness of love and how it can sweep over one. Her recollection of Olivia's behaviour, especially the word 'distractedly', foreshadows the many forthcoming references to madness. Viola captures Malvolio's character perfectly in 'churlish messenger' and sees at the heart of the situation, with a woman's insight of a woman's behaviour, 'the cunning' of Olivia's 'passion' at work. Her moment of epiphany in 'I am the man' leads her to pity Olivia, 'poor lady', and shows her compassion. She now realizes that she is trapped in her disguise, and she also seems to have gained a special knowledge of the way attractive men can deceive impressionable women ('the proper false' setting their forms 'in women's waxen hearts'). She excuses her own and Olivia's weakness at the same time as sadly recognizing her own strange situation, pitying the 'poor monster' she has become. Her 'as I am man', 'as I am woman' formulation of her dilemma is a witty and succinct expression of the complex situation. She ends with a couplet that expresses the spirit of comedy, a mode in which time will untie knotty difficulties if one submits to its untangling power. (This is, of course, the opposite of tragedy, where time is out of joint and amiss and events rush headlong into confusion, death and despair.)

Viola, as Cesario, is able to make things happen. Orsino and Olivia fall in love with her, though the Duke's love runs below the play's surface until the final scene. We watch and hear Olivia fall for Cesario in her very first scene (1.5) and, so long as the actor playing Viola's part possesses the necessary energy and charm, we have no difficulty in understanding how it is that the Countess should be so helplessly captivated. Viola's first achievement is to gain access to Olivia at all (we recall that in the first scene of the play the unsuccessful Valentine returns to Orsino to inform him that he 'might not be admitted, / But from her handmaid do return this answer' (1.1.23–4)). Viola has been admitted due to her persistence and quick-wittedness. Malvolio has found it impossible to dismiss Viola at the gate and returns to Olivia uncertain how to proceed: 'what is to be said to him, lady?'

(1.5.138). Each excuse Malvolio makes is met with Viola's
assumed understanding and 'foreknowledge' (1.5.137) of the situation. Malvolio has returned to tell his mistress that the visitor
is 'fortified against any denial' (1.5.139) and that 'he'll speak with
you, will you or no' (1.5.147). Olivia is already interested, and in
spite of her earlier resolve to admit no representative of Orsino's
she commands Malvolio to 'let him approach' (1.5.156). Why
does Olivia fall in love with Cesario and not his master Orsino?
It is because 'Cesario is so unlike Orsino, so direct and spontaneous, so cheeky, so practical, so real' (Bevington 2002, p. 77).

The way Shakespeare develops his characters here, at the same
time as driving his plot forward, is worthy of close attention, so
let us look in some detail at this crucial scene between Olivia and
Viola in Act 1 Scene 5. The scene begins with Olivia's instruction
to her waiting women to 'Give me my veil, come throw it o'er my
face. / We'll once more hear Orsino's embassy' (1.5.158–9).
Olivia's veil is a token of mourning but also a means of disguise.
So when they first meet both Viola and Olivia are concealing
themselves somewhat, Viola disguised as the male Cesario and
Olivia behind her veil. Viola is determined to cut through the
difficulty of identifying her target audience with a direct question: 'The honourable lady of the house, which is she?' (1.5.160).
Olivia does not make a full disclosure of her identity, though
arguably she gives herself away by speaking at all: 'Speak to me,
I shall answer for her. Your will' (1.5.161). Now begins a curious
device by which Shakespeare brings an absent character, Orsino,
Duke of Illyria, into the scene. Viola begins to speak lines which
are not her own, but learnt from a text, and the text she has learnt
her lines from is Orsino's. However, such is the irrepressible
energy of Viola's own character that she cannot get far into
Orsino's text (a text of rather lame hyperbolic courtly love
poetry) before she interrupts it with her own spontaneous words:

> Most radiant, exquisite, and unmatchable beauty – I pray you
> tell me if this be the lady of the house, for I never saw her. I
> would be loath to cast away my speech, for besides that it is
> excellently well penned, I have taken great pains to con it.
> (1.5.162–6)

The effect of this interruption of herself is enhanced by Shakespeare's theatrical allusions throughout this passage through words such as 'comedian', 'part', 'speech' and 'play':

> Olivia: Whence came you, sir?
> Viola: I can say little more than I have studied, and that question's out of my part. Good gentle one, give me modest assurance if you be the lady of the house, that I may proceed in my speech.
> Olivia: Are you a comedian?
> Viola: No, my profound heart; and yet – by the very fangs of malice I swear – I am not that I play. Are you the lady of the house?
> Olivia: If I do not usurp myself, I am. (1.5.169–78)

This is another victory for Viola, whose directness and persistence has again been rewarded by Olivia revealing her identity. Olivia's interest in the young, sexy visitor is apparent through her personal questioning of him: 'Your will?', 'Whence came you sir?' and 'Are you a comedian?' Though Viola now moves completely out of her prepared text, her exchange of words with Olivia maintains our awareness of the artifice of the situation, for behind Viola and Olivia, and behind Orsino's text, there moves the pen of William Shakespeare, the feigning poet:

> Viola: Most certain if you are she you do usurp yourself, for what is yours to bestow is not yours to reserve. But this is from my commission. I will on with my speech in your praise, and then show you the heart of my message.
> Olivia: Come to what is important in't, I forgive you the praise.
> Viola: Alas, I took great pains to study it, and 'tis poetical.
> Olivia: It is the more like to be feigned, I pray you keep it in. (1.5.179–88)

Olivia is maintaining a disdainful attitude, but Viola's directness and audacity appeal to the Countess and Viola achieves her next success in having Maria and the other attendants dismissed by the increasingly bedazzled Olivia:

Olivia: Yet you began rudely. What are you? What would you?
Viola: The rudeness that hath appeared in me have I learned
from my entertainment. What I am and what I would are as
secret as maidenhead: to your ears, divinity; to any others',
profanation.
Olivia: [to Maria and attendants] Give us the place alone, we
will hear this divinity. (1.5.203–10)

Viola's language here, mixing a sense of conspiracy ('secret') and
sexuality ('maidenhead') with religious devotion ('divinity') and
wickedness ('profanation'), is a potent linguistic cocktail which
works with intoxicating effect on Olivia. Now she knows who
Olivia is and has her alone the scene reverts temporarily to its
origins and Olivia asks Viola: 'Now sir, what is your text?'
(1.5.211). Viola's reply, 'Most sweet lady' (1.5.212), is interrupted by the now impatient Olivia, and the awkwardness of the
next few lines of textual conceit ends with Viola returning to her
strategy of directness with: 'Good madam, let me see your face'
(1.5.220). As Olivia recognizes, Viola is now out of her text, and
this is presumably what appeals to Olivia and leads her to 'draw
the curtain and show you the picture' (1.5.223). By unveiling
here Olivia reveals herself while Viola remains disguised. Not
only does Olivia reveal her physical face, but her comment
immediately following the lifting of the veil ('Look you sir, such
a one I was this present. Is't not well done? (1.5.224)) reveals her
characteristic vanity, a vanity that Viola's reply ('Excellently
done, if God did all' (1.5.226)) undermines by implying that her
beauty may be artificial (owing more to make-up than natural
looks).

Perhaps the most appealing trait of Viola's character is her flex-
ibility, her willingness to adapt to situations – her fleet-mindedness
– and we now have a good example of this capacity of hers to
respond positively and vibrantly to the given situation. Our
impression of some of the other characters of the play is that they
are incapable of such swift transformations, but Viola is more
protean than they, and this is helpful in Illyria. The generosity of
her tribute to Olivia's beauty, as Shakespeare moves her into
poetry for the first time in their encounter, is possessed of a sense

of earnestness, as if spoken from the heart and not as a flattering courtier:

> 'Tis beauty truly blent, whose red and white
> Nature's own sweet and cunning hand laid on.
> Lady, you are the cruell'st she alive
> If you will lead these graces to the grave
> And leave the world no copy. (1.5.228–32)

Viola cuts through Olivia's rather cold prosaic response with further poetry, combining plain-speaking with praise: 'I see you what you are, you are too proud, / But if you were the devil, you are fair' (1.5.239–40), and Olivia finally follows her lead by dropping her flippancy and speaking more truthfully as she too speaks in verse. Though she clearly tells Viola she 'cannot love' Orsino (1.5.246), Viola persists, and in her use of the personal pronoun she bewitches the dazed Olivia: 'If I did love you in my master's flame, / With such a suff'ring, such a deadly life, / In your denial I would find no sense, / I would not understand it' (1.5.253–6). Olivia's enraptured question 'Why, what would you?' completes Viola's line (1.5.256) and brings us to the emotional climax of this scene of first meeting as Viola responds in her own voice:

> Make me a willow cabin at your gate
> And call upon my soul within the house,
> Write loyal cantons of contemnèd love,
> And sing them loud even in the dead of night;
> Halloo your name to the reverberate hills,
> And make the babbling gossip of the air
> Cry out 'Olivia!' O, you should not rest
> Between the elements of air and earth
> But you should pity me. (1.5.257–65)

The brief indications we have had of Orsino's text pale by comparison with Viola's spontaneous and fresh performance, and the tiredness of Orsino's phrasing ought to be highlighted by the passionate delivery required by the actor playing Viola here. Even though she is only expressing what she would do *were* she wooing Olivia, there is more life and emotion in this speech than in all Orsino's stale and unconvincing declarations of love. Viola here, and elsewhere, functions as a dramatic catalyst, creating reactions wherever she goes. She draws both Olivia and Orsino out of themselves. Through her enlivening presence Viola facilitates change in an Illyria populated with stagnant, self-obsessed individuals. The sign that she has altered Olivia through the force of her character is immediate, for as she finishes the 'willow cabin' speech with 'But you should pity me', Olivia responds with 'You might do much. / What is your parentage?' (1.5.266–7). The proud Countess has become captivated, she has caught the plague of love, though we note her concern with social rank even in the moment of falling in love (of which more in Chapter Six on Olivia).

In Act 2 Scene 4 we are presented with Viola attempting to let Orsino know her love, but trapped in her disguise. It is her language which captures Orsino's heart. When asked how he likes the music, 'How dost thou like this tune?' (2.4.18) Viola replies: 'It gives a very echo to the seat / Where love is throned' (2.4.19–20). Orsino's reply, completing Viola/Cesario's half-line, 'Thou dost speak masterly' (2.4.20), is a true compliment. Viola's beautiful expression of the way that music can reflect our inner feelings is reminiscent of Orsino's earlier language in the first scene of the play, though Viola's expression is more succinct, and hence more masterful.

Her eloquence is employed later in the scene to express her own feelings cryptically while gently reprimanding Orsino for his false judgement of women. Her 'Ay, but I know – ' draws Orsino out of his self-indulgent, boastful description of the unparalleled intensity of his love for Olivia and leads him to ask Viola a series of questions: 'What dost thou know?'; 'And what's her history?'; 'But died thy sister?' Viola's responses are curious; both revealing and concealing, they puzzle and enchant Orsino.

Viola: Ay, but I know –
Orsino: What dost thou know?
Viola: Too well what love women to men may owe.
In faith, they are as true of heart as we.

My father had a daughter loved a man
As it might be, perhaps, were I a woman
I should your lordship.
Orsino: And what's her history?
Viola: A blank, my lord. She never told her love,
But let concealment, like a worm i'th' bud,
Feed on her damask cheek. She pined in thought,
And with a green and yellow melancholy
She sat like patience on a monument,
Smiling at grief. Was not this love indeed?
We men may say more, swear more, but indeed
Our shows are more than will; for still we prove
Much in our vows, but little in our love.
Orsino: But died thy sister of her love, my boy?
Viola: I am all the daughters of my father's house,
And all the brothers too; and yet I know not. (2.4.103–21)

Catherine Belsey's comments express some of the puzzlement for the critical reader:

How do the identifications work in this instance? Cesario is Viola and Cesario's father's daughter is Patience who is also Viola. But the equations break down almost at once with, 'what's her history?' 'A blank'. Viola's history is the play we are watching, which is certainly not a blank but packed with events. Nor is it true that she never told her love. She has already told it once in this scene (lines 26–8), and she is here telling it again in hints so broad that even Orsino is able to pick them up once he has one more clue (V.i.265–6). In the play as a whole Viola is neither pining nor sitting, but is to be seen busily composing speeches to Olivia and exchanging jokes with Feste; and far from smiling at grief, she is here lamenting the melancholy which is the effect of unrequited love. (McDonald 2004, p. 646)

The complex effect of the exchange is further complicated by imagining or witnessing performance. A woman, disguised as a man, talks to the man she loves in riddling manner about her sister, which is really herself. She impersonates her brother, who she fears is dead. She knows that the man she speaks to, and loves, loves a woman who loves her. On Shakespeare's stage, in case this were not confusing enough, another layer of complex playfulness existed, for the young woman disguised as a young man is played by a boy!

The vexed situation with Viola/Olivia and Viola/Orsino continues, and so, when we see Viola with Olivia in Act 3 Scene 4 there is a sense of inertia – Viola is still wooing Olivia on Orsino's behalf – Olivia cannot love him and loves Cesario – Viola cannot love her and loves Orsino. She now, though, gets caught up in a plot of Toby's to fight with Aguecheek. This offers some opportunities for sexual innuendo, for example where Viola, in an aside, says 'Pray God defend me. A little thing would make me tell them how much I lack of a man' (3.4.290). There is a quibble here on 'little thing' to refer to the penis she lacks (though the boy actor on Shakespeare's stage would actually have the little thing). There is little development of Viola's character here as she becomes a vehicle for bawdy jokes.

It is not until Antonio enters that Viola again engages with true emotional intensity, responding to Antonio's outburst against her (he mistakes her for Sebastian, with whom he is in love – for further discussion of Antonio and Sebastian see Chapter Eight). We welcome the return of the impassioned Viola, who speaks so feelingly through her rekindled hope: 'Methinks his words do from such passion fly / That he believes himself. So do not I. / Prove true, imagination, O prove true, / That I, dear brother, be now ta'en for you!' (3.4.364–7). The embers of optimism then spark into flame:

> He named Sebastian. I my brother know
> Yet living in my glass. Even such and so
> In favour was my brother, and he went
> Still in this fashion, colour, ornament,
> For him I imitate. O if it prove,
> Tempests are kind, and salt waves fresh in love! (3.4.370–5)

There are associations with Venus here, for Venus was said to have been born from the salty waves of the sea. The emotion is beginning to cascade, building to the crescendo of the final scene.

Viola's description to Orsino of Antonio's behaviour, especially her explanation that "twas but distraction' prepares us for the madness and emotional intensity of the final scene: 'He did me kindness, sir, drew on my side, / But in conclusion put strange speech upon me. / I know not what 'twas but distraction' (5.1.60–2). Viola is confused by Antonio's vehemence and then by Olivia's behaviour. She is then stunned by being addressed by Olivia thus: 'Cesario, husband, stay' (5.1.139). Emotions are high, but there is a farcical quality too. Viola is silent for the most part, and as if not confused enough is then accused by Sir Andrew, who enters bleeding: 'You broke my head for nothing' (5.1.178–9), he complains to her. Viola's increasing astonishment is still building and it reaches its peak with her recognition of, and reunion with, her brother Sebastian. They do not run into each other's arms, but linger in their wonder, exchanging over thirty lines of poetry as the play itself seems to come to an amazed halt.

Viola's final declaration of love (not quite her last words, which are spoken to communicate information about the sea-captain, importantly revealing that Malvolio has had him imprisoned) comes in her penultimate speech. It is a powerful statement of constancy in love: 'And all those sayings will I over-swear, / And all those swearings keep as true in soul / As doth that orbèd continent the fire / That severs day from night' (5.1.263–6). Here Viola speaks masterfully again, though she will soon, when seen in 'other habits', be 'Orsino's mistress' (5.1.377–8). She has reached her 'desirable destination', but, as New Historicist critic Stephen Greenblatt suggestively argues, 'not by pursuing a straight line but by following a curved path' (1988, p. 71). Elliot Krieger's assessment is that while her adoption of a disguise has allowed Viola to 'transform the natural world, whose forces have deprived her of identity and nearly of life, into a playground' (1979, p. 106) she nevertheless 'assumes a subservient position within a functioning society' (p. 107), and this subservience and loss of authority (such as she possesses in her first scene with the captain) leads her into more and more danger. Viola may mediate between Orsino and Olivia with some autonomy but, argues Krieger, this 'dissolves as Orsino incorporates her within his narcissistic fancy' (p. 108). Orsino's threat of violence to Viola in the play's final scene, as a kind of revenge at being spurned by Olivia, is met by Viola's complete surrender: 'And I most jocund, apt and willingly / To do you rest a thousand deaths would die' (5.1.128–9). This is disappointing to the feminist reader, for Viola 'responds to Orsino's whim with total acquiescence; she relinquishes her autonomy by placing her life at the absolute disposal of her master' (Krieger 1979, p. 108). But is Krieger ignoring the erotic suggestiveness of Viola's lines, with their intimation of multiple orgasm ('a thousand deaths would die') in satisfying sexual consummation with Orsino ('To do you rest')?

Imogen Stubbs plays Viola in Trevor Nunn's 1996 film version with a fresh and vivacious energy. Once disguised as a man Stubbs makes an incredibly sexy Cesario and there is an electric edge to certain scenes, most notably in a near kiss with Helena Bonham Carter's Olivia in the scene where they first meet. Her delivery of the 'She never told her love' speech (2.4.110–18) is completely captivating. Comparing Stubbs with Felicity Kendall in the BBC version (1980) we find the latter lacks the conviction and passion that the former possesses.

CHAPTER 4

SIR TOBY BELCH, SIR ANDREW AGUECHEEK AND MARIA

SIR TOBY AND SIR ANDREW

We first see Sir Toby with Maria, and his opening line immediately establishes the carefree nature of his character, though Maria's response presents a less appealing aspect of the knight:

> Sir Toby: What a plague means my niece to take the death of her brother thus? I am sure care's an enemy to life.
> Maria: By my troth, Sir Toby, you must come in earlier a-nights. Your cousin, my lady, takes great exceptions to your ill-hours. (1.3.1–5)

Sir Toby is a fat, drunken sponger, though he is possessed of some charm, and Maria particularly has a soft spot for him (which we learn from Feste when he teases her: 'If Sir Toby would leave drinking thou wert as witty a piece of Eve's flesh as any in Illyria' (1.5.24–6)). This lovable rogue cuts a shabby figure ('These clothes are good enough to drink in, and so be these boots too' (1.3.10–11)) but becomes the central figure of misrule in the carnival atmosphere. It is only as the play draws to a close that we begin to see a less humorous side of Toby's character as his cruelty and bad temper manifest themselves. Early on he is a hugely amusing presence. He preys on Sir Andrew, conning him out of a considerable amount of his money, but we cannot condemn this as Sir Andrew is such a fool, and Sir Toby does bring out Sir Andrew's foolishness as a kind of ridiculous entertainment for the audience. Sir Toby is entirely unapologetic for his habits, and though Maria warns 'That quaffing and drinking will undo you' (1.3.13) Sir Toby soon claims 'I'll drink to her [Olivia, his niece] as long as there is a passage in my throat and drink in Illyria' (1.3.35–7). His lifestyle is one that he seems to feel should be adopted by all: 'He's a coward and a coistrel that will not drink to my niece till his brains turn o'th'toe, like a parish top' (1.3.37–9). The image is suitably frenetic and overwhelming, a figure communicating to us the sense of fleshly appetite conquering the restraining power of reason in a whirling madness.

Before we meet Sir Andrew we have already heard something of him from Sir Toby and Maria. He is 'as tall a man as any's in Illyria' (1.3.17) according to Sir Toby and, more to the point, 'has three thousand ducats a year' (1.3.20). Maria's more sober judgement of him as a 'foolish knight that you brought in one night here to be her wooer' (1.3.14–15) and her later 'He's a very fool, and a prodigal' (1.3.22) sets Sir Andrew's character down for us before his entry, and once he comes on stage we find Maria's opinion verified. Sir Andrew seems incapable of the simplest forms of human communication and his second, third and fourth lines of the play show him in turn unwittingly insulting Maria by referring to her as a 'fair shrew', failing to comprehend Sir Toby's instruction to 'accost' her, and then, seeming to understand, quite mistaking the word 'accost' to refer to Maria's name.

> *Enter Sir Andrew Aguecheek*
> Sir Andrew: Sir Toby Belch! How now, Sir Toby Belch?
> Sir Toby: Sweet Sir Andrew.
> Sir Andrew: [*to Maria*] Bless you, fair shrew.
> Maria: And you too sir.
> Sir Toby: Accost, Sir Andrew, accost.
> Sir Andrew: What's that?
> Sir Toby: My niece's chambermaid.
> Sir Andrew: Good Mistress Accost, I desire better acquaintance.
> Maria: My name is Mary, sir.
> Sir Andrew: Good Mistress Mary Accost. (1.3.41–51)

Sir Toby goes on to explain: 'You mistake, knight. "Accost" is front her, board her, woo her, assail her' (1.3.52–3), but there is very little point in explaining anything to Sir Andrew for, as he himself confesses: 'Methinks sometimes I have no more wit than a Christian or an ordinary man has' (1.3.79–80). Indeed we must concur and go further, judging that Sir Andrew at all times is shown to have far less wit than any other character in Illyria. But put him with his friend, Sir Toby Belch, and Sir Andrew Aguecheek forms one half of a comic double act which provides the audience with plenty of verbal and physical comedy.

Sir Andrew is disappointed in his failure to woo Olivia and is resolved to return home, but Sir Toby is easily able to convince him to stay with a combination of flattery (commenting on his 'excellent' hair (1.3.96)) and misinformation (that he has real hopes with Olivia). Sir Andrew is 'the rich gull of dubious ancestry, a common upstart in Elizabethan London' (Draper 1950, p. 223). Sir Andrew confesses that he is 'a fellow o'th' strangest mind i'th' world' and that he delights 'in masques and revels sometimes altogether' (1.3.105–7) which prompts Sir Toby to egg him on to perform manic and crazy dancing to end the scene: 'let me see thee caper. [*Sir Andrew capers*] Ha, higher! Ha ha, excellent' (1.3.131–2). This physical humour is of course dependent for its effect on the particular performer and it is crucial therefore that the actor playing Sir Andrew is capable of capering in a sufficiently absurd and amusing manner so as to elicit laughs from the general audience, and not merely from the flattering Sir Toby.

As Sir Andrew demonstrates his abilities in various forms of dancing Sir Toby encourages him with phrases designed to lead him to further and further idiocy; however, while some of Sir Toby's references invite specific and speculative interpretations, other phrases can be seen as expressing general themes of the play:

Wherefore are these things hid? Wherefore have these gifts a curtain before 'em? Are they like to take dust, like Mistress Mall's picture? Why dost thou not go to church in a galliard, and come home in a coranto? My very walk should be a jig. I would not so much as make water but in a cinquepace. What

dost thou mean? Is it a world to hide virtues in? I did think by
the excellent constitution of thy leg it was formed under the
star of a galliard. (1.3.117–25)

Though Toby's questions, 'Wherefore are these things hid?' and
'Is it a world to hide virtues in?', seem to gently mock Sir Andrew,
nevertheless his dancing has the virtue of entertaining and thus
we detect an echo of the instruction Jesus makes that one's light
should not be put 'under a bushel, but on a candlestick; and it
giveth light unto all that are in the house. Let your light so shine
before men, that they may see your good works, and glorify your
Father which is in heaven' (Matthew 5.15–16). Even at the height
of physical humour in the play, then, there is a more profound
wisdom operating.

We next meet Sir Toby in Act 1 Scene 5, and he is 'half-drunk'.
At this point his drunkenness is amusing. His mistaken use of
'lechery' for 'lethargy' (1.5.120) entertains, but a tone of solem-
nity creeps in when Olivia asks Feste: 'What's a drunken man
like, fool?' (1.5.124).

Feste: Like a drowned man, a fool, and a madman: one
draught above heat makes him a fool, the second mads him,
and a third drowns him.
Olivia: Go thou and seek the coroner, and let him sit o' my coz,
for he's in the third degree of drink, he's drowned. Go look
after him.
Feste: He is but mad yet, madonna, and the fool shall look to
the madman. (1.5.125–30)

Toby is a burden to Olivia and his dissolute behaviour, while
entertaining for a while, soon palls. Drinking, foolishness and
madness are shown in Feste's logic to follow one from the other,
sequentially.

In Act 2 Scene 3 Sir Toby is in his element. He is up late with
Sir Andrew and they meet Feste to carry on drinking and generally carousing. They sing and cavort, and then Malvolio interrupts them. It is the clash of Carnival and Lent, and Toby
represents the Carnival. He speaks for all revellers as he puts

down Malvolio: 'Art any more than a steward? Dost thou think because thou art virtuous there shall be no more cakes and ale?' (2.3.106–8). The forces of festivity are in the ascendant, with the plot to humiliate Malvolio developing as soon as he has been seen off here. However, the scene ends with a reminder of Sir Toby's exploitation of Sir Andrew in which we might recognize a precursor of the relationship Shakespeare was to put on stage a couple of years later in the tragedy of *Othello*, the relationship between Iago and Roderigo. Iago is always telling Roderigo to 'Put money in thy purse' and we see Toby opting for the same strategy of repetition (and tempting the dupe through promise of the satisfaction of desire, also a tactic of Iago's):

> Sir Toby: She's a beagle true bred, and one that adores me. What o'that?
> Sir Andrew: I was adored once too.
> Sir Toby: Let's to bed, knight. Thou hadst need send for more money.
> Sir Andrew: If I cannot recover your niece, I am a foul way out.
> Sir Toby: Send for money, knight. If thou hast her not i'th'end, call me cut.
> Sir Andrew: If I do not, never trust me, take it how you will.
> Sir Toby: Come, come, I'll go burn some sack, 'tis too late to go to bed now. Come knight, come knight. (2.3.167–79)

It is apparent that Sir Toby has a soft spot for Maria and she for him. Always inventive linguistically, Sir Toby has many names for Maria as, for example, at 2.5.12 where he greets her: 'Here comes the little villain. How now, my metal of India.' In the box-tree Toby tries not to boil over at Malvolio's impertinence. He cannot hold the peace, though Malvolio does not hear his outraged utterances. He is well pleased with the gulling of Malvolio and seems to marry Maria on the strength of it. When he says, 'I could marry this wench for this device' (2.5.171), the idiotic Sir Andrew characteristically echoes him: 'So could I too' (2.5.172). This is daft enough, but in pushing the stupidity of Sir Andrew ever further Shakespeare achieves high levels of comic absurdity:

Sir Toby: And ask no other dowry with her but such another jest.

Enter Maria

Sir Andrew: Nor I neither.

Fabian: Here comes my noble gull-catcher.

Sir Toby: [*to Maria*] Wilt thou set thy foot o' my neck?

Sir Andrew: [*to Maria*] Or o' mine either?

Sir Toby: [*to Maria*] Shall I play my freedom at tray-trip, and become thy bondslave?

Sir Andrew: [*to Maria*] I'faith, or I either? (2.5.173–81)

Here, the fool, the gull, is clearly Sir Andrew who, without an original thought in his head, tries to involve himself with the fun and games.

Though he may echo scripture in Act 1 Scene 3, as discussed above, it is Sir Toby who moves the joke on Malvolio forward to another, more sinister and disturbing level, when he announces to Maria in Act 3 Scene 4:

Come, we'll have him in a dark room and bound. My niece is already in the belief that he's mad. We may carry it thus for our pleasure and his penance till our very pastime, tired out of breath, prompt us to have mercy on him, at which time we will bring the device to the bar and crown thee for a finder of madmen. (3.4.130–5)

Before we become too outraged, however, at Toby's suggestion we ought to observe that this was the 'usual treatment for madness' (Donno 1985, p. 113). Toby's speech here raises many of the play's concerns: madness, pleasure, penance, pastimes, appetite and excess, and mercy. There is an odd concept of mercy at work here though, mercy that is prompted by exhaustion only. But with Sir Toby and Sir Andrew there is a sense of exhaustion, especially in the build-up to the duel between Sir Andrew and Viola which seems laboured and full of needlessly garrulous speeches. Part of the problem seems to be with Toby's loquaciousness. There is a glimpse of the collapse of the alliance between Sir Toby and Sir Andrew that is to come when Toby, speaking to Fabian, speaks in a candid manner which allows us to see his true feelings of disdain for his 'friend': 'For Andrew, if he were opened and you find so much blood in his liver as will clog the foot of a flea, I'll eat the rest of th'anatomy' (3.2.57–9). This leaves us with an image of the man of unrestrained appetite, Sir Toby, literally devouring Sir Andrew.

After all their fooling around it is perhaps shocking to us that Sir Toby turns on Sir Andrew in the play's final scene. It is a very cruel moment, certainly the cruellest in their relationship, as Toby, suffering from a head wound inflicted by Sebastian, rejects Sir Andrew in no uncertain terms. Sir Andrew, rather touchingly we feel, is trying to assist his friend, but in reply to his 'I'll help you, Sir Toby, because we'll be dressed together' (5.1.197–8) (meaning that they will have their wounds dressed together), Sir Toby fires a barrage of abuse: 'Will *you* help – an ass-head, and a coxcomb, and a knave; a thin-faced knave, a gull?' (5.1.199–200). The jovial mask has slipped, and our final impression of the life and soul of the festivities is of a bad-tempered rogue, a fraudulent drunkard. We perhaps wonder about the future happiness of Toby and Maria, reflecting on Toby's previous cruelty and our enjoyment of it. In his penultimate line Shakespeare has Sir Toby condemn himself out of his own mouth as he complains about Dick Surgeon, who Feste has informed him is drunk. 'I hate a drunken rogue' (5.1.195), says Sir Toby churlishly. The last laugh is most certainly on him.

Ought we to be shocked by Toby Belch's vicious outburst against Andrew Aguecheek? The director Bill Alexander's production of *Twelfth Night* at Stratford-upon-Avon in 1987 presented the brutality of much of the play's comedy and represented the relationship between Sir Toby and Sir Andrew as a sadomasochistic one, with Toby manipulating and bullying a Sir Andrew who seemed to enjoy the treatment. In conversation with Michael Billington and other directors of *Twelfth Night*, a conversation set down in print in a book which provides the reader with plenty of food for thought concerning the problems faced and solutions offered by those who actually stage the play, Bill Alexander states:

I think Sir Toby is a frankly sadistic individual [. . .] Sir Toby represents a classic, red-necked, cock-fighting, bear-bating, stone-throwing Elizabethan who ruthlessly manipulates a daffy person because he wants to get money out of him. That sadism is there and has to be shown. I don't think softening it enhances the comedy or the romance or the charm of the play, although the tendency is to want to soften things. (Billington 1990, pp. 56–7)

Though John Caird, director of a 1983 *Twelfth Night* with the Royal Shakespeare Company, also involved in the conversation, agreed with Alexander that 'there is nothing jolly about Sir Toby at all [. . .] He is vicious almost to the point of being sadistic at times, but he is also a very sad man' (Billington 1990, p. 58), nevertheless he makes a vital point, and that is that 'there is so much life in Toby', that he is 'the man who says, "Come on. Just because you are like you are doesn't mean there won't be cakes and ales. We will not put up with this deadly atmosphere. We're going to celebrate. We're going to live"' (ibid). John Barton, another director of the play, thinks that the 'sado-masochistic label is a dangerous one, because it implies a psychopathology, which is not present in this comedy' (ibid, p. 59). Barton is right to object to psychopathological labelling of dramatic characters, though the preying behaviour of Toby is carefully shown by Shakespeare. Toby may be full of life but we see his mean side, for example, in an aside where he says of Sir Andrew: 'I'll ride your horse as well as I ride you' (3.4.279).

As the holiday excesses of the play end it is not surprising that Sir Toby is more and more ill at ease. His rampant irresponsibility in the earlier part of the play, caring for nothing but the feeding of his own insatiable appetite, is punished in the final scene as he enters having received a head wound from Sebastian. We come to see the essential selfishness of Toby's character and to understand what Krieger points out:

Sir Toby's freedom from time does not, in short, replace permanent everyday responsibility with the temporary holiday celebration of good fellowship; rather, Sir Toby's holiday depends on *his* permanent freedom from responsibility. He uses the mechanisms of revelry and celebration so as to create a private and fundamentally selfish world. (1979, pp. 102–3)

After Toby's final exit Fabian informs us that Maria forged Olivia's hand in the letter to Malvolio 'at Sir Toby's great importance, / In recompense whereof he hath married her' (5.1.354–5). So Toby ends the play married to Maria, though she is strangely absent from the play's final scene.

MARIA

Maria impersonates Olivia by imitating her characters (letters) in the letter for Malvolio. Toby describes her as 'Penthesilea' (Queen of the Amazons) and 'a beagle true bred' (a reference to her tenacity and size, for the beagle is a small hunting dog) (2.3.165–7). Maria is motivated by a desire for 'revenge' (2.3.142), and she seems determined to prove her wit in the trick on Malvolio. She is not able to face up to Malvolio openly, only uttering 'Go shake your ears' (2.3.117) after he has left. Draper sees Maria as characterized by 'loyalty and discretion', 'feminine guile' and 'quick-witted cleverness' (1950, p. 224) and we can see all these qualities at work in this scene. However, she is also vengeful and quite nasty. After Malvolio has read her forged letter and, following the instructions in the letter, started to behave in a ridiculous fashion, she reports this to Sir Toby with some relish, a little pride and some slightly worrying undercurrents of fantasies of violence:

I have dogged him like his murderer. He does obey every point of the letter that I dropped to betray him. He does smile his face into more lines than is in the new map with the augmentation of the Indies. You have not seen such a thing as 'tis. I can hardly forbear hurling things at him. I know my lady will strike him. If she do, he'll smile, and take't for a great favour. (3.2.70–7)

It is she who instructs Feste in the goading of the imprisoned Malvolio, providing him with gown and false beard (which she later comments he might have done without as Malvolio 'sees thee not' (4.2.65)). She orders Feste to 'Do it quickly. I'll call Sir Toby the whilst' (4.2.2–3). She seems determined to impress Sir Toby with her tricks and schemes, but by this stage he is tiring of the sport. She is, it seems, a small woman, for Viola jokes about her being a giant, and refers to her as 'good swabber' (1.5.195) in an effective put-down. Sir Toby also refers to her as 'the youngest wren of nine' (3.2.62), which is explained as a reference to 'the youngest hatched, and so supposedly the smallest, of the brood of the smallest bird' (Warren, p. 165). However, the Folio text has 'mine', not 'nine', and this would indicate Toby claiming posses-sion of Maria. Either way, the reference is clearly made to her diminutive size. Hotson offers the most audacious reading of Maria's smallness. He points out that 'the tiny wren is both uni-versally known as King of the Birds, and connected with this feast [the Feast of Light and of the Three Kings held on Twelfth Night] in a fashion as familiar as it is baffling' (1954, p. 160). Hotson, a mine of fascinating contextual information for any student of Shakespeare's *Twelfth Night*, also makes the grand claim that it is not Feste or Sir Toby Belch who presides as the Christmas festival Lord of Misrule:

> On the contrary, it is the quick, deviceful, strong-brained little gentlewoman, Maria, whom Shakespeare sets up as rightful ruler of the sport royal, and she richly deserves her crown at the Buttery-bar as a finder of madmen. His excellent ground for this – and, as we have seen, for the choice fitness of the play's main plot as well – is the date of his production, 1600: leap year, women's year. 'Dian doth rule, and you must dom-ineer.' Inevitably Maria reigns as Lady of Misrule, and inevitably she hooks and lands her fish, Toby. (Hotson 1954, p. 159)

Though looking at the play from a different perspective, a Marxist one, Elliot Krieger also singles out Maria for special mention when he claims that of all the characters in the play only she 'indicates the bourgeois and Puritan emphasis on independence, competition, and the association of stature with merit' (1979, p. 121). This might surprise the reader who judges Malvolio to represent 'the spirit of bourgeois independence' (p. 121). We will have more to say on Malvolio in this regard when we look at his character in Chapter Seven. As for Maria, we can clearly see her as a character who does use her wits to displace Malvolio, her rival, and who achieves her desire in marrying Sir Toby, whom she impresses with her ability. By marrying Sir Toby she marries into Olivia's family and is 'freed from the consequences of duplicity toward her mistress' (Krieger 1979, p. 120).

The casting of Toby, Maria and Andrew is strikingly successful in Trevor Nunn's film version, with Sir Toby played by Mel Smith, Maria by Imelda Staunton and Sir Andrew by Richard E. Grant. The scenes of slapstick humour and drunkenness are hilariously rendered by Smith and Grant. Staunton's Maria is a thoroughly convincing 'beagle true bred' in her tenacious gulling of Malvolio. The rejection of Aguecheek by Belch is indeed moving, as Grant slinks off despondently, providing a distraction that helps to prolong the recognition of Viola by Sebastian.

CHAPTER 5

FESTE (AND FABIAN)

THE CLOWN RETURNS

Feste arrives on stage with Maria in Act 1 Scene 5 of the play and we quickly learn that he is in trouble with Olivia. We seem to be hearing them in mid-conversation, and the melancholic mood is firmly set with talk of hanging:

> Maria: Nay, either tell where thou hast been or I will not open my lips so wide as a bristle may enter in way of thy excuse. My lady will hang thee for thy absence.
> Feste: Let her hang me. He that is well hanged in this world needs to fear no colours. (1.5.1–5)

Feste's absence is worth commenting upon, as it is reiterated by Maria a few lines on: 'Yet you will be hanged for being so long absent, or to be turned away – is not that as good as a hanging to you?' (1.5.15–17). We are, it seems, encouraged to ponder Feste's absence which, though only reported, strangely makes his presence more felt. Clowning has been missing from Olivia's household, and now it returns and, by way of following Maria's instruction to 'make your excuse wisely' (1.5.28), Feste teases the grieving Olivia into better spirits. Feste's reference to fearing no colours has also introduced another sombre aspect of the play as 'colours' is a proverbial reference to the flags and standards of war, and Maria makes this clear to us by explaining its derivation. Feste then utters a line which accentuates one of the notable oppositions in the play, wisdom and foolishness: 'Well, God give them wisdom that have it; and those that are fools, let them use their talents' (1.5.13–14). Shakespeare drives home the idea of the topsy-turvy nature of the world of his play with Feste's further elaboration on the matter a few lines on:

> Wit, an't be thy will, put me into good fooling! Those wits that think they have thee do very oft prove fools, and I that am sure I lack thee may pass for a wise man. For what says Quinapalus? 'Better a witty fool than a foolish wit.' (1.5.29–33)

Though we have already had a brief taste of his wit in his exchange with Maria we now see Feste in full flow, audaciously confronting Olivia and, far from apologizing for his long absence, attacking her for her foolish mourning:

> Olivia: (*to attendants*) Take the fool away.
> Feste: Do you not hear, fellows? Take away the lady.
> Olivia: Go to, you're a dry fool. I'll no more of you. Besides, you grow dishonest. (1.5.34–7)

But Feste's insistence, coupled presumably with a charisma that Olivia finds difficult to resist, leads Olivia to tolerate his presence and to hear his proof that she is a fool:

> Feste: Good madonna, why mourn'st thou?
> Olivia: Good fool, for my brother's death.
> Feste: I think his soul is in hell, madonna.
> Olivia: I know his soul is in heaven, fool.
> Feste: The more fool, madonna, to mourn for your brother's soul being in heaven. Take away the fool, gentlemen. (1.5.61–7)

This is not merely a 'proof' that Olivia is a fool, but evidence of Feste's wit and charm. Olivia is impressed and, although Maria feared she would at the very least dismiss her clown, we find her reflecting on his healing influence and asking Malvolio whether he agrees. Malvolio's reply to her question makes clear an opposing view of Feste:

Olivia: What think you of this fool, Malvolio? Doth he not mend?
Malvolio: Yes, and shall do, till the pangs of death shake him. Infirmity, that decays the wise, doth ever make the better fool. (1.5.68–72)

Feste does indeed 'mend', though we could argue that he also rends. The bitterness of this attack on his character from Malvolio simmers through the play, resurfacing at the end with his chilling lines to the humiliated steward: 'but do you remember, "Madam, why laugh you at such a barren rascal, an you smile not, he's gagged" – and thus the whirligig of time brings in his revenges' (5.1.364–7). This suggests a vengeful Feste who harbours a grudge and reminds his victim of the repayment for past injuries, though there are other interpretations possible (see Warren, p. 67). Feste is not a simple clown figure. Though his name suggests a festival figure he remains somewhat detached from the action, somehow not really participating while at the same time setting the mood for the play (which, as we have seen in our discussion of Orsino and Viola, is something that can be claimed for other characters).

Of Feste, Michael Billington asks: 'What is the key line about him? Is it that he is a corrupter of words?' (1990, p. 63) and we see him fulfilling this function particularly effectively in the scene where he claims this of himself, a scene in which he and Viola exchange some droll witticisms:

Enter Viola as Cesario and Feste the clown, with [pipe and] tabor
Viola: Save thee, friend, and thy music. Dost thou live by thy tabor?
Feste: No, sir, I live by the church.
Viola: Art thou a churchman?
Feste: No such matter, sir. I do live by the church for I do live at my house, and my house doth stand by the church.
Viola: So thou mayst say the king lies by a beggar if a beggar dwell near him, or the church stands by thy tabor if thy tabor stand by the church.

Feste: You have said, sir. To see this age! A sentence is but a chev'rel glove to a good wit, how quickly the wrong side may be turned outward. (3.1.1–13)

There is a tiredness about the humour here; the wordplay seems somewhat hollow and incapable of raising laughter. The dialogue seems designed to lead into a reflection on the very nature of punning humour. And Feste links these reflections to the age itself, as if the capacity to turn language inside out were a sickness of the time, an indication, or a product, or perhaps even a cause, of a peculiar disease in Elizabethan culture. In response to Viola's fairly innocent enquiry as to whether Feste is Olivia's fool, Feste gives the following answer:

No indeed sir, the Lady Olivia has no folly, she will keep no fool, sir, till she be married, and fools are as like husbands as pilchards are to herrings – the husband's the bigger. I am indeed not her fool, but her corrupter of words. (3.1.31–5)

The reference to 'chev'rel gloves', gloves made of a 'very soft, pliable leather easily turned inside out, is an apt expression for the way in which a phrase can be manipulated for witty purposes' (Warren, p. 153). The idea of corruption that Feste brings in with his comment works as a subtle confession from Shakespeare concerning the wicked sleight of hand of the playwright/wordsmith. In a counterbalancing move, however, after Feste's exit here, Shakespeare gives Viola a speech in which she makes a vital comment on Feste, a comment which we must take, coming as it does from Shakespeare's perceptive heroine, as indicative of the essence of Feste's (and by inference the actor's and the playwright's) character:

This fellow is wise enough to play the fool,
And to do that well craves a kind of wit.
He must observe their mood on whom he jests,
The quality of the persons, and the time,
And like the haggard, check at every feather
That comes before his eye. This is a practice

As full of labour as a wise man's art,
For folly that he wisely shows is fit,
But wise men, folly-fall'n, quite taint their wit. (3.1.59–67)

Viola's speech draws attention not only to the wisdom of the fool, but also to his function as entertainer, and to the stresses and strains of being a jesting player. Feste is a performer, and requires payment for his performances. He entertains with his wit, but also with his musical abilities, through instrument and voice. He has four solo songs in the play, each in a different style. His first song is performed for Sir Andrew Aguecheek and Sir Toby Belch, who are up late after a night of heavy drinking and fully intend to drink and carouse further. As versatile as a jukebox, Feste gives them a choice: 'Would you have a love-song, or a song of good life?' and they both agree on the former. Feste obliges with a performance of a carpe-diem lyric that they find 'Excellent good' (2.3.43). The second verse particularly strikes home, both for his ageing on-stage audience, and for those gathered in the theatre to watch and hear what they might have thought was going to be a light-hearted comedy but which, by this stage in the proceedings, they must feel to be patched together with a persistent fabric of melancholy:

O mistress mine, where are you roaming?
O stay and hear, your true love's coming,
    That can sing both high and low.
Trip no further, pretty sweeting.
Journeys end in lovers meeting,
    Every wise man's son doth know.

What is love? 'Tis not hereafter,
Present mirth hath present laughter.
    What's to come is still unsure.
In delay there lies no plenty,
Then come kiss me, sweet and twenty.
    Youth's a stuff will not endure. (2.3.37–42, 45–50)

'O mistress mine' may be a traditional song, but the words are thought to be Shakespeare's own, and given to Feste they suggest an insight not possessed of other characters. The first stanza seems to refer to Olivia and Viola/Cesario, who can 'sing both high and low'. The second stanza strikes a more general tone of regret at time's passage and the inevitability of age (a sentiment particularly suited to his audience on stage, who are themselves no longer 'sweet and twenty'). Feste's 'mellifluous voice' (2.3.51) and 'contagious breath' (2.3.52) is so catching that Sir Toby suggests a 'catch' to 'rouse the night-owl' (2.3.55–6). Feste's singing here brings pleasure and unity to the scene.

Perhaps the most surprising of Feste's songs is 'Come Away Death', which injects, right in the heart of this festive comedy, a dose of morbid realism about the transitory nature of life and love. Feste performs it for the love-sick Duke and the Duke's future wife, disguised as Cesario, the hopelessly and secretly in love (with Orsino himself) Viola:

> Come away, come away death,
>   And in sad cypress let me be laid.
> Fie away, fie away breath,
>   I am slain by a fair cruel maid.
> My shroud of white, stuck all with yew,
>   O prepare it.
> My part of death no one so true
>   Did share it.
>
> Not a flower, not a flower sweet
>   On my black coffin let there be strewn.
> Not a friend, not a friend greet
>   My poor corpse, where my bones shall be thrown.
> A thousand thousand sighs to save,
>   Lay me O where
> Sad true lover never find my grave,
>   To weep there. (2.4.50–65)

There is a danger at this point, if the song is sung expertly and fittingly enough, that the play drowns in melancholy. The mercenary Feste is pleased to receive his reward and, it seems, wittily squeezes two gifts of money from the (one assumes moved)

Orsino. We may assume that Orsino is moved by the song, and Viola too, but what of Feste? He seems remarkably detached, as a truly professional performer should be, wryly commenting on the inconstant nature of the Duke before departing with a simple 'farewell' (2.4.77). And Shakespeare allows him to maintain a distance from the central levity (if later problematic) of the play, the gulling of Malvolio, by introducing a new character in the form of Fabian (see the end of this chapter for a brief discussion of Fabian).

Feste's parody of the gospel story of the talents, when he tells Maria, 'God give them wisdom that have it; and those that are fools, let them use their talents' (1.5.13–14), is an early example of one of Feste's talents, as noted by the Oxford editors, namely to employ a 'mock-religious phrasing', and this 'reaches its climax in his impersonation of Sir Topaz (4.2)' (Warren, p. 103). In that later scene, where Malvolio is cruelly tormented by the increasingly malevolent Feste, he announces his arrival at the prison in a mocking reference to the Elizabethan *Book of Common Prayer* of 1559, which Shakespeare and his audience would have known well. In that book there is a particular section giving instructions for the proper form of words to be employed when visiting the sick. The entry reads thus: 'The order for the Visitation of the Sick. When any person is sick, notice shall be given thereof to the Minister of the Parish; who, coming into the sick person's house, shall say, Peace be to this house, and to all that dwell in it.' Feste, clearly mocking this ritual, approaches Malvolio with these words: 'What ho, I say, peace in this prison.' His next utterances can be seen as further scriptural parody, now of Matthew 17.15 in which a man kneels down before Jesus and says, 'Lord, have mercy on my son: for he is lunatick, and sore vexed.' Feste's lines clearly echo this when he answers Malvolio's 'Who calls there?' (4.2.21) with 'Sir Topaz the curate, who comes to visit Malvolio the lunatic' (4.2.22–3) and in his next utterance in which he considers Malvolio to be possessed: 'Out, hyperbolical fiend, how vexest thou this man!' (4.2.26). It is Feste who plays the devil that vexes Malvolio here, horribly travestying the instructions from the order for the visitiation of the sick, which ends with 'A Prayer for persons troubled in mind or in conscience', which itself ends with the following words, words which would be familiar to Shakespeare and his audience and which, in their shocking contrast to his behaviour here, suggest the wickedness and profanity of Feste's tormenting of the troubled Malvolio: 'Deliver him from fear of the enemy, and lift up the light of thy countenance upon him, and give him peace, through the merits and meditation of Jesus Christ our Lord. Amen.' Topaz is a precious stone which was thought in Elizabethan times to have curative properties, especially in cases of madness (Warren, p. 192), which adds to the malicious mockery by Feste in this scene.

Feste, far from healing or curing or comforting the ailing Malvolio, seems bent on driving him mad and undermining his faith. In the exchange, for example, concerning Pythagoras, Feste says he will only admit Malvolio is sane when he 'shalt hold th'opinion of Pythagoras' (4.2.58) concerning the transmigration of human souls into different kinds of bodies, an opinion which no believer of Christian doctrine could hold. Malvolio has all too sanely already explained to Feste: 'I think nobly of the soul, and no way approve his opinion' (4.2.55). Feste is relentless here. Though one might see his agreement to fetch 'light, and paper, and ink' (4.2.118) for Malvolio and to take his letter to Olivia as an act of some kindness, we must note that it is not until Malvolio has promised that 'It shall advantage thee more than ever the bearing of letter did' (4.2.112–13) that he finally agrees.

Even Feste's song has a sinister and cruel impact here. When he employs his own voice, as instructed by Sir Toby, Feste begins with a song which seems designed to mock Malvolio, for the unkind Olivia loves another, Cesario. In a deft touch from Shakespeare his song is punctuated by Malvolio's cries of 'fool' from his cell. The effect would be hard to imagine as pleasing in any way either to Malvolio or the audience in the theatre.

Feste: (*sings*) 'Hey Robin, jolly Robin,
Tell me how thy lady does.'
Malvolio: Fool!
Feste: 'My lady is unkind, pardie.'
Malvolio: Fool!
Feste: 'Alas, why is she so?'

Malvolio: Fool, I say!
Feste: 'She loves another.' (4.2.72–9)

Feste concludes this most disturbing scene with a further song, for which no music survives. This song seems Feste's darkest moment, where he explicitly links himself to 'the old Vice' of the medieval morality plays, a precursor of the Elizabethan fool. The song seems somewhat mad in itself, and it is difficult to discern a clear meaning here, but the 'rage' and 'wrath' mentioned suggest Feste's 'mad lad' performance as frenzied and crazed, designed to madden Malvolio, and it ends by casting Malvolio as 'goodman devil'. Thus the traditional morality play feature of the old Vice mocking the devil becomes the Elizabethan festival jester Feste ridiculing the darkly imprisoned 'kind of puritan' Malvolio:

I am gone, sir,
And anon, sir,
    I'll be with you again,
In a trice,
Like to the old Vice,
    Your need to sustain,
Who with dagger of lath
In his rage and his wrath
    Cries 'Aha' to the devil,
Like a mad lad,
'Pare thy nails, dad,
    Adieu, goodman devil.' (4.2.121–32)

The delivery of Malvolio's letter to Olivia is far from hasty; indeed Feste gives it to her only after Olivia has ordered that they 'Fetch Malvolio hither' (5.1.272) and, having admitted that he 'should have given't you today morning' (5.1.280), he does his utmost to undermine the level-headedness of the contents of the letter with his refusal to read it in a sensible voice. His argument is that 'I do but read madness' (5.1.287) and that 'to read his right wits is to read thus' (5.1.290–1). Olivia's patience is finally exhausted and she instructs Fabian to read the letter instead.

This is a significant moment, and helps to explain the importance of the presence of Fabian both to the play and to the maintenance of a special kind of detachedness from all others for the character of Feste. One thinks that Olivia might repeat one of her earliest lines to Feste at this point: 'Now you see, sir, how your fooling grows old, and people dislike it' (1.5.105–6).

Though madness seems rife in this play, Feste, it seems, only plays the madman when he decides to. His early comment to Olivia should be remembered as an indication of his clear-mindedness: 'Lady, *cucullus non facit monachum* – that's as much to say as I wear not motley in my brain' (1.5.50–1). He, like Viola, is not truly what he plays. Feste plays the patched fool, he plays the ranting madman, he even plays the (malevolent) monk in the form of Sir Topaz (4.2) (the meaning of the Latin above is 'the cowl does not make the monk' (Warren, p. 105)), but he never plays himself, he remains unknown and unknowable, and that is because he is a player whose 'character' is only an impression we develop of this essentially enigmatic figure.

Let us remember that Feste himself informs Viola, and us, that he is not Olivia's fool 'but her corrupter of words' (3.1.34–5). He alerts us to the slipperiness of language, and we would be unwise, or foolish, to forget his warning as we read or listen to Shakespeare's rhetorically dazzling text, always in the mouth of another, always concealing the author's real self or character. We might ask whether Feste is a voice of truth or a puzzling enigma. Krieger sees him as a man who serves others to serve himself. He notes that Feste 'demands and receives material reward from nearly all of the aristocrats in the play' (Krieger 1979, p. 115) and this is certainly true. Feste gets money out of Sir Toby and Sir Andrew (2.3.30–3), Orsino (2.4.66–8 and 5.1.23–43), Viola (3.1.42–52) and Sebastian (4.1.18). Though we do not see Feste directly extracting money from Olivia, we see him as generally dependent on her. Krieger goes on to make a telling comparison: 'Feste's nearly obsessive concern with payment for services forms an obvious and absolute contrast with Viola's attitude toward material compensation' (1979, p. 115). The example cited is Viola's response to Olivia's offer of payment for delivering Orsino's message: 'I am no fee'd post, lady, keep your purse. / My

master, not myself, lacks recompense' (1.5.274–5). Viola's
response denotes her as an aristocrat rather than a servant. One
simply cannot imagine Feste refusing such an offer of money.

We end our discussion of this intriguing character with a consideration of his final song:

> When that I was and a little tiny boy,
>   With hey, ho, the wind and the rain,
> A foolish thing was but a toy,
>   For the rain it raineth every day.
>
> But when I came to man's estate,
>   With hey, ho, the wind and the rain,
> 'Gainst knaves and thieves men shut their gate,
>   For the rain it raineth every day.
>
> But when I came, alas, to wive,
>   With hey, ho, the wind and the rain,
> By swaggering could I never thrive,
>   For the rain it raineth every day.
>
> But when I came unto my beds,
>   With hey, ho, the wind and the rain,
> With tosspots still had drunken heads,
>   For the rain it raineth every day.
>
> A great while ago the world begun,
>   With hey, ho, the wind and the rain,
> But that's all one, our play is done,
>   And we'll strive to please you every day. *Exit* (5.1.379–98)

There has been extensive comment on this song. Hotson remarks
that 'For lack of understanding its drift, this song has naively
been received as a tale in rime but little reason: nonsense con-
temptible or nonsense charming; but nonsense' (1954, p. 167). He
asks whether Feste is a man 'to waste his wit in nonsense? He
knows precisely what to provide as a fitting farewell to wassail and
saturnalian excess: and it is not something adapted to a Christmas

party for Victorian young persons' (p. 167). This is rather a coy way of putting it, but further on Hotson speaks more plainly: 'Feste has already given us his exquisite love songs; now we are to be sent away with "a song of good life". What he trolls out is a Drunkard's Progress' (p. 170). The Oxford editors provide a helpful analysis of this song, in which they argue that it serves as 'a kind of epilogue' (Warren, p. 70). Lois Potter expresses the effect of the end of the song well: 'at the end of his song the singer turns himself back into a performer – not a solitary figure, but a member of a company of actors who "strive to please you every day" ' (1985, p. 33). The Oxford editors state that in his final verse Feste seems 'about to offer us more stern truths about the world – but then, with a general evasiveness that may perhaps be a final reflection of the play's elusiveness, he appears to change his mind, breaks off, and instead offers us a courteous farewell as he eases us out of the world of the play' (Warren, p. 73).

Ben Kingsley, who plays Feste in Trevor Nunn's 1996 film version of the play, portrays the character with memorable intensity. He is a Feste for our age, with a sense of menace conveyed, a mellifluous voice and a confident detachment and independence, tinged with melancholy throughout. The final image of the film, with Kingsley's Feste spinning away down the hillside, echoes again the whirligig of time which, as we have seen, will bring in 'his revenges'. This complicates Feste's parting laughter and the final lines of his song. In what way will Feste strive to please us 'every day' (repeated three times here)? Perhaps the enigmatic clown strives to please as an agent of time's vengeful whirligig, by visiting us and taunting us in our dark tormented cells of unrequited love.

WHY FABIAN?

Fabian has been seen by many as a weakness in the play. We will allow Billington to represent these voices with his series of questions, and then we will consider some possible answers:

> Would you say that the character of Fabian is proof of Shakespeare's genius as a playwright, or of his occasional

incompetence? Suddenly, half way through *Twelfth Night*, a totally unexplained character called Fabian joins the action and becomes part of the plot against Malvolio. Who is Fabian? Where has he come from? Why is he there? (Billington 1990, p. 101)

Earlier in this chapter Fabian's introduction was explained as a device whereby Shakespeare can remove Feste from the central joke of the play. Warren and Wells speculate on Shakespeare's intention in introducing Feste: 'perhaps he wanted to maintain Feste's detachment as an ironic commentator, or perhaps he decided not to involve him in the earlier stages of the plot so that his eventual participation, in the Sir Topaz scene, will have maximum impact' (Warren, p. 53). Both these suggestions seem plausible, though we can never be sure of authorial intention. What we can more helpfully examine is the effect of Fabian's introduction, which is indeed to allow Feste to detach himself somewhat from the action. The only reliably true answer to Billington's questions is: Fabian is a character who is there because Shakespeare decided he should be. As with other characters we can look at what he says and does. If we do this we find that he is a very useful character in terms of widening the sense of grievance against Malvolio, but also the sense of the cruelty of Elizabethan society (at least in our minds, for which of us would not side with Malvolio against the cruel 'sport' of bear-baiting?).

Fabian's presence is sufficiently explained in his first two lines:

Enter Sir Toby, Sir Andrew, and Fabian
Sir Toby: Come thy ways, Signor Fabian.
Fabian: Nay, I'll come. If I lose a scruple of this sport let me be boiled to death with melancholy.
Sir Toby: Wouldst thou not be glad to have the niggardly rascally sheep-biter come by some notable shame?
Fabian: I would exult, man. You know he brought me out o' favour with my lady about a bear-baiting here.
Sir Toby: To anger him we'll have the bear again, and we will fool him black and blue, shall we not, Sir Andrew? (2.5.1–9)

The effect of this need not be awkward, but adds to the sense that we develop of a gathering of animals who scent blood and want to play their part in the sport of taking down the bugbear Malvolio. Fabian is the latest dog to join the salivating pack. His part in the action is often functional: another body is needed on stage during the duel between Sir Andrew and Cesario, for example, and he is given a memorable line which draws full attention to the artifice of the theatre and serves as a pre-emptive strike against any who would claim that Shakespeare's crazy world of Illyria is unreal by admitting it to be so: 'If this were played upon a stage now, I could condemn it as an improbable fiction' (3.4.122–3).

Fabian replaces Feste in the reading of Malvolio's letter as the fool's mad antics fail to amuse. Fabian's function as an agent of disclosure continues in his speech at 5.1.346–59 in which he attempts to gloss over events, suggesting that things are evened up 'If that the injuries be justly weighed / That have on both sides passed' (5.1.358–9). He refers to the spirit with which the trick was played on Malvolio as 'sportful malice' (5.1.356) and argues that it 'may rather pluck on laughter than revenge' (5.1.357). But there is no laughter at this point, none whatsoever. The treatment of Malvolio looks far more like 'malice' than sport and is now far from funny. And it is not laughter but revenge, both fulfilled and promised, that ends the play.

CHAPTER 6

OLIVIA

GRIEF AND LOVE

We first hear of Olivia in the first scene of the play, where Orsino casts her as Diana to his Actaeon:

> O, when mine eyes did see Olivia first
> Methought she purged the air of pestilence;
> That instant was I turned into a hart,
> And my desires, like fell and cruel hounds,
> E'er since pursue me. (1.1.18–22)

This is a powerful image of the suffering lover and the idealized beloved and, according to the critic Leslie Hotson, could be considered a crucial key to the interpretation of the entire play (Hotson 1954, pp. 123–36). Even without Hotson's historical researches a knowledge of the myth referred to here denotes Orsino's sense of distance from Olivia, that she is somehow unattainable and that his desire for her will be self-destructive. For the story of Actaeon and Diana (Artemis in the Greek), well known in Elizabethan England, tells of the wrath of the goddess who was

> incensed at having been seen naked by Actaeon when she was bathing in a spring. The goddess incited his pack of fifty hounds to fury and she set them on him. They ate him without recognizing him, then hunted for him in vain

throughout the forest, which echoed with their howls. (Grimal 1986, p. 10)

It is a story, then, of male inferiority and voyeurism; of female divinity and cruelty; of driven obsession leading to self-annihilating grief. It is a myth with patterning importance for Shakespeare's comedy.

We do not have long to dwell on the image, however, for Valentine, one of Orsino's attending gentlemen, immediately enters and informs Orsino that he has failed to gain admission to Olivia, returning with a message 'from her handmaid' to his love-lorn lord. This 'answer' to Orsino's suit creates an impression of an Olivia who, like her suitor, is characterized by excess and artifice:

> The element itself till seven years' heat
> Shall not behold her face at ample view,
> But like a cloistress she will veilèd walk
> And water once a day her chamber round
> With eye-offending brine – all this to season
> A brother's dead love, which she would keep fresh
> And lasting in her sad remembrance. (1.1.25–31)

Olivia's nun-like state is a withdrawal from the world which seems extreme, even morbid, and some of Valentine's language suggests this. The 'eye-offending brine' which is used 'to season / A brother's dead love' presents us with an image of Olivia pickling her dead brother in her tears, as if to preserve him ('keep fresh / And lasting'). The eye which is offended is perhaps not just Olivia's, but the imaginative observer of this macabre ritual. In *Twelfth Night* love is for the living, not the dead, and Olivia's fixation on her brother's 'dead love' clearly cannot be allowed to stand. It is Viola though, not Orsino, who will cause her to change her behaviour and remove her veil, and it is Viola, herself disguised as Cesario, who will draw her into love and into the light, leaving thoughts of her dead brother behind.

We first see Olivia in Scene Five of the play when she enters with Malvolio and other attendants to confront the long-absent clown, Feste. Her first line is an order to 'Take the fool away' (1.5.34), but rather than this leading to the removal of Feste we witness him proceeding to prove her a fool for mourning a brother whom she believes to be in heaven. Olivia finds Feste's wit somewhat healing, but Malvolio, her steward, disagrees, and Olivia is left attempting to mediate between them with a diplomatically balanced judgement: 'There is no slander in an allowed fool, though he do nothing but rail; nor no railing in a known discreet man, though he do nothing but reprove' (1.5.88–91). When she is then informed by Maria that 'there is at the gate a young gentleman much desires to speak with you' (1.5.94–5) she is concerned to discover that it is Sir Toby, her kinsman, who holds this visitor 'in delay' (1.5.99) and she immediately instructs Maria to 'Fetch him off, I pray you, he speaks nothing but madman. Fie on him.' (1.5.101–2). Thus far we are presented with an Olivia who is trying to keep order but who evidently has difficulties in imposing her authority on her household. She has lost a brother, and before him a father, and is now the lady of the house; however, she appears to be surrounded by individuals who seem determined to follow their own paths rather than subjugate their desires to her will. In the figure of Olivia, Shakespeare presents us with a woman confronting the problems of female rule.

Into this already rather unruly household comes Viola, disguised as Cesario and presenting the figure of 'a fair young man' (1.5.97), according to Maria. Reports from Malvolio of the insistence and persistence of this young man interest Olivia sufficiently for her to 'Let him approach' (1.5.156), ostensibly to 'once more hear Orsino's embassy' (1.5.159) but, we suspect, more out of a kindling interest in this 'very well-favoured' (1.5.153) young man. The ensuing scene shows Olivia metamorphosing from mourning sister to rapt lover, and sustains the theme of changeability established in Viola's disguise as Cesario and Orsino's fickle and impermanent character. Olivia's transformation is swift and total, though not magical, for the only charm at work is Viola's audacious performance, which cuts through Olivia's pride and forces her out of her dismal grief. As she herself questions, 'How now? / Even so quickly may one catch the plague?' (1.5.284–5).

The 'eye-offending brine' (1.1.29) has dried up and Olivia can now speak lines which suggest a new flood of emotion: 'Methinks I feel this youth's perfections / With an invisible and subtle stealth / To creep in at mine eyes. Well, let it be' (1.5.286–8). Her stubborn grief has been miraculously replaced with a desire to surrender to the commands of love.

Olivia has, in a very real sense, lost control of herself, and she gives this fact memorable expression in the pair of couplets which bring to a close this charming scene: 'I do I know not what, and fear to find / Mine eye too great a flatterer for my mind. / Fate, show thy force, ourselves we do not owe. / What is decreed must be; and be this so' (1.5.298–301). And so the first scene in which we meet Olivia leaves her entirely changed. She begins the scene attempting to mediate and to rule her household and ends it submitting to fate with a resigned reminder to us all of the commandments of love. In Illyria, characters are compelled to realize the truth of Olivia's 'ourselves we do not owe' (with 'owe' meaning 'own'), and are forced to succumb to the overwhelming power of desire. And Olivia is unable to conceal this change in her entirely, for Maria later comments that 'Since the youth of the Count's was today with my lady she is much out of quiet' (2.3.123–4).

When Orsino sends Cesario again to woo Olivia he describes her as 'yon same sovereign cruelty' (2.4.79), a comment which tells us more about his disappointment than her character. She is evidently beautiful, as we have seen and heard in Act 1 Scene 5, and Orsino claims that it is 'that miracle and queen of gems / That nature pranks her in attracts my soul' (2.4.84–5). His love, he grandly states, is 'more noble than the world' (2.4.80). This language of Orsino's concerning Olivia is devalued in the play and we essentially come to see it as false. It is the language of courtly love, the language of poetic wooing, and to be viewed with suspicion. (This courtly love language of Orsino's has been discussed earlier in Chapter Two.) Viola has, for her first encounter with Olivia, learnt Orsino's lines, and begins to deliver them. She says that she has taken 'great pains to study' the message from Orsino, 'and 'tis poetical' (1.5.186). Olivia's reply is withering and dismissive of such poetry: 'It is the more like to

be feigned, I pray you keep it in' (1.5.188). She is far more interested in the messenger than the message: 'I heard you were saucy
at my gates, and allowed your approach rather to wonder at you
than to hear you' (1.5.189–91).

Jean Howard offers a coherent feminist reading of Olivia in
her article 'Crossdressing, the Theatre, and Gender Struggle in
Early Modern England'. Howard writes:

> At the beginning of the play [Olivia] has decided to do without
> the world of men, and especially to do without Orsino. These
> are classic marks of unruliness. And in this play she is pun-
> ished, comically but unmistakably, by being made to fall in
> love with the cross-dressed Viola. The good woman, Viola,
> thus becomes the vehicle for humiliating the unruly woman in
> the eyes of the audience. (Howard 1988, p. 432)

But is Olivia really humiliated by Viola? Might falling in love
with the cross-dressed Viola be an erotic adventure, or as Olivia
puts it, 'a most extracting frenzy of mine own' (5.1.275), that
leads her out of her cloistered mourning and into a new life?
Indeed, Olivia seems to be rewarded for her passion by the convenient arrival of Sebastian to balance the equation.

Howard's 'humiliated' seems too strong, but Olivia does give
voice to sensations of a ferocious kind. Surprisingly, she uses an
image to describe her situation which Shakespeare presents at
various points in his text, an image taken from the terrible
Elizabethan 'sport' of bear-baiting, in which bears were shackled
to a stake and fighting dogs were set on them for the entertainment of the betting public. Olivia admits that she sent her ring
after Cesario/Viola 'in a shameful cunning' (3.1.114) and then
she passionately asks to know Viola's thoughts, employing this
violent (and perhaps slightly erotic) image of submissiveness to
Viola's dominant force:

>   What might you think?
> Have you not set mine honour at the stake
> And baited it with all th'unmuzzled thoughts
> That tyrannous heart can think? To one of your receiving

Enough is shown. A cypress, not a bosom,
Hides my heart. So let me hear you speak. (3.1.115–20)

She is exposed, figuratively and perhaps somewhat literally, before her new love. Not only Viola's thoughts but Olivia's too are becoming 'unmuzzled'. It is an image that reminds us of Orsino's description in the play's first scene, of his desires pursuing him 'like fell and cruel hounds', an image which expresses the overwhelming power of erotic feeling, while simultaneously suggesting anguish, pain and suffering.

Amongst all the memorable characterization, music and mayhem of the comedy it may be missed that, as Draper has it, 'the major plot of *Twelfth Night* is clearly the story of Olivia and her four or five lovers: Orsino, Sir Andrew, Malvolio, and Viola-Sebastian' (1950, p. 215). The positioning of Olivia as central to the plot means that the way she is played has a huge impact on the mood of a production. Billington writes that 'stage tradition always had insisted that Olivia was a grave, mature woman' (1990, p. xvii), and he quotes John Wain's opinion that 'Shakespeare made Olivia a countess full of authority and aristocratic hauteur' (p. xviii). ('Hauteur', by the way, is a 'loftiness of manner or bearing' (*OED*).) The evidence of the play suggests otherwise, and indeed more recent film and stage performances present us with a younger, sexier Olivia. Olivia does fall in love with Viola with a passionate intensity suggestive of youthfulness, and her hasty marriage to Sebastian suggests impetuous and impatient desire rather than 'authority' and 'hauteur'. Peter Hall's production of the play in 1958 is seen as changing the way Olivia was portrayed for the better. Hall took a 'radical decision' to cast Geraldine McEwan in the role. McEwan was a popular West End actress in her mid-twenties and she portrayed Olivia as a 'pouting, giggling, squealing' young woman who was 'bored to death with acting the role of the great lady' and who was 'erotically stirred by Cesario' (Billington 1990, pp. xvii–xviii).

Olivia in Trevor Nunn's 1996 film is played by a young Helena Bonham Carter, opposite a younger Imogen Stubbs as Viola. Bonham Carter's Olivia is indeed, it seems, 'erotically stirred' by Stubbs's Viola, and the air crackles between them in a highly charged moment in the scene in which they first meet where they appear to be about to kiss. The scene is played and directed with consummate skill. Their hair seems to touch even though their lips do not. And then Olivia is drawn out into the garden, followed by Cesario/Viola, imagining him/herself in his/her master's place, and Olivia plays along, falling in love, catching the plague: 'Why, what would you?' (1.5.257) she asks Viola/Cesario. Cesario's passion (or is it Viola's?), and the threat of that passion to the status quo, is summed up in a quick clip of the surprised Malvolio hearing the exuberant (and loud) 'Olivia' hallooed by Stubbs. Viola's outburst shocks Bonham Carter's Olivia into an open-mouthed, open-eyed awe, suggestive of the love-struck, astonished state she is now in. This Olivia is well stirred and well shaken. It is a clear turning point in the drama, signalled by an intercut image of Malvolio stopping in his official tracks at the sound of Viola's 'Olivia', and making an about-face turn for the film audience.

Though there is a disturbing amount of cruelty in the play, Olivia seems untainted. She may suffer in her own frustrated desire for Cesario, but at no point does she appear malevolent or vindictive. She seems genuinely concerned for Malvolio at the end of the play, regretting that her own preoccupations have led her to forget his predicament: 'A most extracting frenzy of mine own / From my remembrance clearly banished his' (5.1.275–6). Olivia has been the victim of the practical joke too. Her hand-writing has been forged by Maria; her hospitality has been abused by her drunken uncle Toby and his idiot friend, Sir Andrew; her authority has been undermined and not a little mocked by Maria, Feste, Belch, Aguecheek and Fabian; her steward has been imprisoned in darkness under false pretences, and efforts have been made to drive him out of his wits. Olivia refers to him as 'poor gentleman' (5.1.274) and, on discovering the full truth from an understandably impassioned Malvolio, she responds with grace and pity, promising that 'when we know the grounds and authors of it / Thou shalt be both the plaintiff and the judge / Of thine own cause' (5.1.344–6). After Malvolio leaves the stage, with threats of revenge ringing in everyone's ears, it is only Olivia who expresses a concern proportionate to the wrong done to him. Shakespeare places the very same phrase in her mouth that Malvolio himself used in the prison scene, as if to give it special emphasis: 'He hath been most notoriously abused' (5.1.369). It is her last line of the play, and, along with her penultimate line, 'Alas poor fool, how have they baffled thee!' (5.1.360), leaves us with an impression of her compassionate humanity. No other character in the play expresses such regret at Malvolio's treatment.

This concern for Malvolio is a good example of Olivia's involvement in the world of love and care. Krieger point out 'a unique stage direction in Shakespeare's works – "*clock strikes*"' (3.1.127). This takes place during a scene between Olivia and Viola (as Cesario), and Krieger argues that her response, 'The clock upbraids me with the waste of time' (3.1.128), signals a new attitude to time. Whereas at the beginning of the play she had time to mourn her dead brother for seven years, by the end of the play there is an urgency in her actions (consider how hastily she marries Sebastian) as if she had woken up to the fact of time's passage. As Krieger has it: 'By the end of the drama Olivia's private second world has dissolved into a world of community, the world of time' (1979, p. 104).

To conclude this chapter we look at perhaps the most challenging and challenged idea concerning the play, an idea put forward by Leslie Hotson in his 1954 book *The First Night of Twelfth Night*. Hotson's claim, which is dismissed by most critics, is that the play was written for a particular occasion and a particular audience. He traces many, many textual clues, and develops his reading carefully throughout his fascinating book, which reads more like a detective story than a volume of literary criticism. Hotson argues that in writing *Twelfth Night* Shakespeare set out to please Queen Elizabeth, his most significant audience member.

> Indeed in the art of subtle and delicate compliment Shakespeare is able to give the courtiers lessons, as he proves again and again while painting – in that 'virtuous maid' Lady Olivia – a romanticized and youthful shadow of 'the most excellent and glorious person of our sovereign the Queen'. (Hotson 1954, p. 121)

As part of his analysis of the play, Hotson ingeniously argues that the character of Olivia is a tribute to Elizabeth. Olivia has a name in which the 'quick, resourceful, and allusive' Elizabethan mind would detect a connection between the olive branch, an emblem of 'triumphant peace', and their queen (Hotson records that two portraits of Elizabeth 'after the Armada show her sceptred with a branch of olive, "the badge of peace, the ensign of true love"' (Hotson 1954, p. 122)). Furthermore, Hotson states that 'Live!' or 'O live!' is the 'universal shout of [Elizabeth's] loving subjects' (p. 122). At the start of this chapter we remarked on the first mention of Olivia by Orsino in which he defined himself as Actaeon to her Diana. This fits with Hotson's analysis, for Diana, chaste goddess of the hunt and the moon, was frequently employed by Elizabethan poets as a mythological rendering of their virgin Queen. But Hotson does not rest there; he goes further:

> Shakespeare takes little pains to mask his allusions to the listening Sovereign Lady Elizabeth in the person of Lady Olivia, queen in her Illyrian house. He portrays a *sovereign cruelty*, whose heart might be supplied with one self *king*. To both Feste and Viola she is a *princess*. And in matters of state, Lady Olivia falls naturally into the royal *we*: 'We'll once more hear Orsino's embassy', 'Give us the place alone: we will hear this divinity', 'We will draw the curtain and show you the picture', 'But when we know the grounds and authors of it'. Moreover she wields a power of life and death impossible to any countess. Maria warns Feste 'My lady will hang thee', and Olivia commands, 'Hold, Toby! On thy life I charge thee hold!' (p. 126)

This is intriguing evidence indeed, and it does not require one to accept all of Hotson's extended, detailed argument to find him convincing on the link between Olivia and Elizabeth. If Hotson is correct, it certainly must affect one's interpretation of the play generally, and of Olivia in particular. We will return to Hotson's thesis in the Conclusion, but for now it is worth remarking that it is rewarding to consider Hotson's analysis for, as the Oxford editors state, although 'his main argument has not won general acceptance', nevertheless 'his book sheds much valuable light on details of the text', from which the excellent commentary in their edition has, they acknowledge, 'benefited' (Warren, p. 4).

CHAPTER 7

MALVOLIO

OLIVIA'S STEWARD

Malvolio's first words are an attack on Feste and reveal a bitterness and envy in his character that sours his world:

> I marvel your ladyship takes delight in such a barren rascal. I saw him put down the other day with an ordinary fool that has no more brain than a stone. Look you now, he's out of his guard already. Unless you laugh and minister occasion to him, he is gagged. I protest I take these wise men that crow so at these set kind of fools no better than the fools' zanies. (1.5.78–84)

Olivia's reply puts Malvolio firmly in his place and, perhaps more than any other comment by him or about him, fixes his character in our minds: 'O, you are sick of self-love, Malvolio, and taste with a distempered appetite' (1.5.85–6). Olivia, we must assume, is well acquainted with Malvolio, and this judgement of the steward, coming from her, is borne out by what we subsequently witness. Appetite – for music, for food, for drink, for love, for life – is a key theme of the play, and Olivia's statement neatly establishes Malvolio as the enemy of the pleasures of indulging one's appetite. The steward of Olivia's household is predisposed to savour the bitter side of life and to disapprove of those who see life as a great feast of the senses.

Olivia sends Malvolio after Cesario with a ring that she claims he has left behind with her. Malvolio is useful to Olivia in this way, but he allows his distempered appetite to develop ideas about Cesario which go beyond Olivia's description of what has occurred. Thus it is that Malvolio responds with ill-temper to Cesario's 'She took the ring of me. I'll none of it', a comment that shows the quick-thinking Viola, 'sensitive to Olivia's predicament, dissemble in the presence of her messenger' (Donno 1985, p. 71). Malvolio addresses Viola with 'Come sir, you peevishly threw it to her, and her will is it should be so returned' (2.2.13–14), and with this he '*throws the ring down*'. The difference in the two characters, Viola and Malvolio, could not be greater here. Viola is capable of 'quickly sizing up the situation', and 'with characteristic generosity she conceals Olivia's rash indiscretion from her steward' (Warren, p. 46). Though brief, this 'tiny exchange points the difference between an ungenerous nature and a generous one with brilliant economy' (Warren, p. 46). It is not Viola/Cesario who is peevish here, but Malvolio, again accentuating the negative.

Malvolio's next entry brings him into direct conflict with Sir Toby, Sir Andrew, Maria and Feste as he tries to break up their loud, drunken, post-midnight revelry:

> My masters, are you mad? Or what are you? Have you no wit, manners, nor honesty, but to gabble like tinkers at this time of night? Do ye make an ale-house of my lady's house, that ye squeak out your coziers' catches without any mitigation or remorse of voice? Is there no respect of place, persons, nor time in you? (2.3.81–7)

Malvolio is doing his duty here as a steward, protecting his mistress's house from the manic excesses of Sir Toby and friends. In 1595 the Second Viscount of Montague, a young nobleman called Anthony Browne, set down some of the responsibilities of an Elizabethan steward. Browne explained that

> the steward should 'in civil sort' reprehend and correct 'negligent and disordered persons', reforming them by his 'grave admonitions and vigilant eye', among these the 'riotous, the contentious, and quarrelous persons of any degree' as well as

'the frequenters of tabling, carding and dicing in corners and at untimely hours and seasons'. (Donno 1985, p. 13)

Though Malvolio is attempting to keep order as a steward should, he does not do so 'in civil sort'. His language is derisive, even offensive. To say that they 'gabble like tinkers' is a particularly strong put-down for Malvolio to use to his social superior Sir Toby, for the term tinker 'was synonymous with "vagrant" or "gypsy"'(Warren, p. 128) and in some places in England (Banbury for instance) tinkers were hanged by puritan town councils (Hotson 1954, p. 101). When Sir Toby responds by effectively telling him to go hang ('Sneck up!' (2.3.88)), Malvolio targets him with a specific threat from Olivia:

> Sir Toby, I must be round with you. My lady bade me tell you that though she harbours you as her kinsman she's nothing allied to your disorders. If you can separate yourself and your misdemeanours you are welcome to the house. If not, an it would please you to take leave of her she is very willing to bid you farewell. (2.3.88–94)

After the ring scene with Viola, where Malvolio goes beyond Olivia's language, putting his own negative spin on the situation, we wonder whether Malvolio misrepresents Olivia. Has she really bade Malvolio to threaten Sir Toby with eviction? Sir Toby seems unfazed, though Maria tries to calm him down, but Malvolio remains snootily unimpressed by Toby's continuing antics and interjects a sarcastic 'This is much credit to you' (2.3.101). After Toby's decisive attack on his rank, 'Art any more than a steward?' (2.3.106), Toby delivers the trumpet-blast against the puritan Lenten force of Malvolio: 'Dost thou think because thou art virtuous there shall be no more cakes and ale?' (2.3.107–8). So saying, Toby cuts to the heart of the problem with Malvolio: he thinks he is virtuous – actually he is as lustful, proud, arrogant and self-centred as any person in Illyria. But more damning than all these common faults is the fact that Malvolio is a hypocrite. Toby launches a further attack on Malvolio's status with 'Go sir, rub your chain with crumbs'

(2.3.111–12), a derogatory reference to the crumbiness of Malvolio's office, and follows this up with a call for 'A stoup of wine Maria' (2.3.112). This prompts Malvolio to threaten Maria personally before exiting: 'Mistress Mary, if you prized my lady's favour at anything more than contempt you would not give means for this uncivil rule. She shall know of it, by this hand' (2.3.113–16). Her parting shot, 'Go shake your ears' (2.3.117), may be another reference to bear-baiting in the play (of which more in the Conclusion), and if so seems to cast Malvolio as the blood-soaked bear. Robert Langham's account of entertainments at Kenilworth Castle in 1575 contains a description of a baited bear who is said to 'shake his ears twice or thrice with the blood and slaver about his physiognomy' (Warren, p. 130). It is worth remarking here, in this chapter devoted to Malvolio, that Shakespeare seems keen to link Toby, Maria and Aguecheek, and later Fabian, with the blood sport of bear-baiting in this play. Indeed, we could see Malvolio as becoming the bear for these bloodthirsty dogs to attack.

Maria's ensuing description of Malvolio seems essentially accurate. First she suggests that 'sometimes he is a kind of puritan' (2.3.130). Commentators have made much of this, though we should note Maria's 'sometimes'. When she further describes Malvolio we learn that he is only a puritan when he chooses to be, that he is essentially inconstant (we have seen that constancy/inconstancy is a theme of the play) and, as Olivia has already suggested, that he is a conceited egotist who thinks far too highly of himself:

> The dev'l a puritan that he is, or anything constantly but a time pleaser, an affected ass that cons state without book and utters it by great swathes; the best persuaded of himself, so crammed, as he thinks, with excellencies, that it is his grounds of faith that all that look on him love him; and on that vice in him will my revenge find notable cause to work. (2.3.136–42)

Maria's reference to 'physic', or medicine, 'I know my physic will work with him' (2.3.160–1), is picked up by Draper, who argues

that 'above all, Malvolio's moving passion betrays his choleric nature' (1950, p. 103). Draper goes on to argue that the first half of the play 'presents Malvolio's choleric malady' while the second half 'shows how those about him, either with a witting malice like Maria and Sir Toby, or with an unwitting regard, like Olivia, undertake to "Physicke" this malady, or at least curb its extremes' (p. 108). It does seem clearly established by this point that Malvolio, in the carnival atmosphere of *Twelfth Night*, needs to be taken down a peg or two, and what better way but to play on his self-love and fool him into thinking that he might be on the rise, even to the giddy heights of Olivia's bedchamber?

Our next sight of Malvolio confirms Olivia's and Maria's analysis of his character, for he speaks to himself while his enemies hide and the device of the soliloquy allows us to know his ridiculously high opinion of himself even before the discovery of the letter designed to work on his vanity. Malvolio appears here 'crammed, as he thinks, with excellencies' (2.3.139–40), as Maria has said, and he is clearly ripe and ready to interpret Maria's imitation of Olivia's hand in the most flattering light:

'Tis but fortune, all is fortune. Maria once told me she did affect me, and I have heard herself come thus near, that should she fancy it should be one of my complexion. Besides, she uses me with a more exalted respect than anyone else that follows her. What should I think on't? (2.5.21–6)

Indeed, his next utterance conveys the height of his ambition: 'To be Count Malvolio!' (2.5.32). His fantasy continues, and all before the discovery of the letter, with an amusing role-play of himself as Count Malvolio, lording it over Sir Toby, an imagined elevation in rank made all the more amusing by the fact that the concealed Toby must subdue his natural inclination to riotous outrage and remain undetected. Malvolio thinks of himself 'calling my officers about me, in my branched velvet gown, having come from a day-bed where I have left Olivia sleeping' (2.5.44–6), and goes on to envisage Toby approaching and curt-seying: 'I extend my hand to him thus, quenching my familiar smile with an austere regard of control [. . .] saying "Cousin

Toby, my fortunes, having cast me on your niece, give me this pre-rogative of speech" – [. . .] "You must amend your drunken-ness" ' (2.5.62–9). Malvolio's horrendous and intolerable self-importance here ironically makes him the most hilarious figure in the play. He projects a sombre and serious restraint and control but actually exhibits some of the most exaggerated excesses we see in the play. It is fitting, therefore, that he becomes the butt of the joke, though the excesses of the baffling of Malvolio in turn mean that the sense of sympathy swings like a pendulum back toward the hapless steward. Certainly with his imprisonment, Malvolio ceases to be the 'overweening rogue' (2.5.27) of the early part of the play and becomes instead a man whom Olivia judges 'hath been most notoriously abused' (5.1.369). But at this point in the play we can only laugh at the excesses of Malvolio's smug self-satisfaction:

> O ho, do you come near me now? No worse man than Sir Toby to look to me. This concurs directly with the letter, she sends him on purpose, that I may appear stubborn to him, for she incites me to that in the letter. 'Cast thy humble slough,' says she, 'be opposite with a kinsman, surly with servants, let thy tongue tang arguments of state, put thyself into the trick of singularity', and consequently sets down the manner how, as a sad face, a reverend carriage, a slow tongue, in the habit of some sir of note, and so forth. I have limed her, but it is Jove's doing, and Jove make me thankful. And when she went away now, 'let this fellow be looked to'. Fellow! – not 'Malvolio', nor after my degree, but 'fellow'. Why, everything adheres together that no dram of a scruple, no scruple of a scruple, no obstacle, no incredulous or unsafe circumstance – what can be said? – nothing that can be can come between me and the full prospect of my hopes. Well, Jove, not I, is the doer of this, and he is to be thanked. (3.4.62–80)

Shakespeare's characterization of the oily steward here is mag-nificent and his 'lubricious self-projection, cunningly revealed in a day-dream-like soliloquy, is splendidly comic' (Donno 1985, p. 13). The speech surely does cause us to laugh, but it also reveals an unpleasant predatory egotism in Malvolio, even though he claims that all 'is Jove's doing'. His 'I have limed her', an image referring to the Elizabethan practice of catching birds by placing birdlime, a sticky substance, on twigs and branches, thereby entangling them, linguistically links Malvolio to the tyrannous Claudius in *Hamlet*, who says: 'O limed soul that struggling to be free / Art more engaged' (*Hamlet* 3.3.68). The comparison of the uses of this term presents Claudius in the more favourable light, as a man who speaks eloquently of the human condition. Malvolio's 'I have limed her' sounds sinister, not only arrogant, but suggestive of a premeditated manipulation of the vulnerable Olivia into a trapped submission to her steward. Terry Hands detects this premeditation in Malvolio's behaviour:

> The moment we got Malvolio on stage we'd see he was putting up blocks against anybody else getting to Olivia. He pushes aside Feste, and he is extremely upset that there is a ring being sent to Cesario, to the point where he leaves it on the floor rather than actually handing it over. And he is trying to push Toby and Ague-Cheek out of her care. Whatever means he is using, the actual mechanism in front of your eyes is that there is this man, who is close to her, and who is doing his damnedest to stop anybody else getting anywhere near her. (Billington 1990, p. 83)

Maria's 'physic' is powerful in its effect on Malvolio, bringing out the worst in him. His overwhelming sense of superiority comes to the fore and he desires no one's company but his own (and perhaps Olivia's). He tries to dismiss Fabian, Toby and Maria with disdain: 'Go off, I discard you. Let me enjoy my private. Go off.' (3.4.86–7) and later, after they goad him with the suggestion that he is possessed by the devil, he parts from them saying: 'Go hang yourselves all. You are idle shallow things, I am not of your element. You shall know more hereafter' (3.4.118–20). Toby's comment that 'His very genius hath taken the infection of the device' (3.4.124), with its use of the term 'genius', alerts us to the deep-seated impact of the forged-letter plot on Malvolio's character. The word 'genius' is variously glossed as 'nature' or 'tutelary spirit (or angel) guarding an individual' (Donno 1985, p. 112); 'soul (literally "attendant spirit")' (Warren, p. 175); 'soul, spirit; literally, familiar or guardian spirit' (Lothian and Craik 1975, p. 100). The idea that Malvolio's very nature, spirit, soul has been infected by the 'device' of their practical joke is perhaps the beginning of the shift in audience sympathy towards the misled steward. Indeed, the plot against Malvolio takes a sinister turn in Toby's next utterance: 'Come, we'll have him in a dark room and bound' (3.4.130). The demonization of Malvolio makes all treatment of him possible, and the joke now develops into an intention, it seems, to drive Malvolio completely mad.

The play is at its darkest, and the treatment of Malvolio at its cruellest, in Act 4 Scene 2 where we find Malvolio imprisoned 'in hideous darkness' (4.2.31). Malvolio claims that 'never was man thus wronged' (4.2.29). In reply to Feste, disguised as the curate Sir Topaz, claiming that 'there is no darkness but ignorance' (4.2.43–4), Malvolio speaks feelingly, maintaining an insistence on his sanity in the most trying of circumstances: 'I say this house is as dark as ignorance, though ignorance were as dark as hell; and I say there was never man thus abused. I am no more mad than you are. Make the trial of it in any constant question' (4.2.46–9). But Feste refuses the 'constant question', or 'consistent, logical discussion' (Warren, p. 194) that Malvolio requests, insisting instead that Malvolio will not be considered sane and be released until he agrees with the Pythagorean belief in the transmigration of souls, a form of heresy for a Christian. The tormenting of Malvolio here is not just in the form of his dark imprisonment, but also in the psychological mind-games that seem designed to drive him from his wits. Malvolio achieves our admiration by his laudable fortitude in suffering, by his refusal to go mad. In his dark prison Malvolio manages, once Feste brings him the candle, pen, ink and paper that he so rationally requests, to write a letter to Olivia which, given his situation, is a masterpiece of restraint and civility. It is through the eloquence of his characters (letters) on paper that Malvolio will first speak in the play's final scene, when his letter to Olivia is read aloud.

MALVOLIO AS A TRAGIC FIGURE

By the final scene we are so far from the levity of the earlier trick, the laughter of the joke, that the carnival atmosphere has been replaced with a wholly different mood. There is hard talk from Olivia, who seeks to redress the injustice done to Malvolio by promising that he will be 'the plaintiff and the judge / Of thine own cause' (5.1.345–6), but this is not sufficient to mollify him. By now we have come to understand why William Hazlitt wrote: 'We feel a regard for Malvolio, and sympathise with his gravity, his smiles, his cross garters, his yellow stockings, and imprisonment' (Palmer 1972, p. 32). Paul Edmondson argues that 'Fabian's reading of the letter is crucial, as it can establish the audience's sympathy for Malvolio before he finally appears' (Edmonson 2005, pp. 161–2). Malvolio's letter does give him a presence in the scene before he enters. Letters are a way of bringing characters onto the stage when they are not physically present, and not through others talking about them, but giving them their own voice (to an extent, for someone else has to read the letter). In this instance it is Fabian who reads (after Feste refuses to read in any other voice than his imitation of a madman). Malvolio's character is thus presented through his characters (written inscriptions) on the page of writing. His letter, soberly read by Fabian, serves as a dignified prologue to Malvolio's entrance:

> By the Lord, madam, you wrong me, and the world shall know it. Though you have put me into darkness and given your drunken cousin rule over me, yet have I the benefit of my senses as well as your ladyship. I have your own letter that induced me to the semblance I put on, with the which I doubt not but to do myself much right or you much shame. Think of me as you please. I leave my duty a little unthought of, and speak out of my injury.
> The madly used Malvolio. (5.1.293–302)

In Bill Alexander's 1987 *Twelfth Night*, with Antony Sher as Malvolio, 'you could see that he was totally enslaved by Olivia by the way he rushed off to rinse her tear-stained handkerchief under the village pump and by his unnerving habit of popping up from behind walls like a private eye every time she cried "what ho"' (Billington 1990, p. xxviii). For Billington, 'the real controversy centred on the final scenes, which Mr Sher played as if Malvolio had been driven out of his wits: in the prison-scene he was tethered to a stake by a halter and he was last seen essaying cross-gartered kicks as if totally deranged' (p. xxviii). This seems a mistaken interpretation for, as we have seen in the evidence of his behaviour in the cell, his letter and his rational responses in the play's final scene, Malvolio remains completely sane. He may suffer a temporary 'midsummer madness' (3.4.53) earlier in the play, when he believes Olivia to be in love with him, but his sobering experience in the cell has washed that completely out of his brain. After his letter is read out, Orsino comments, 'This savours not much of distraction' (5.1.305), and Olivia immediately orders Malvolio's release: 'See him delivered, Fabian, bring him hither' (5.1.306). The two highest-status figures in the play judge, from his letter alone it seems, that Malvolio is not, indeed, insane.

Leslie Hotson mounts a case for reading Malvolio as a 'prime jest, pleasant and without scurrility, audacious without impudency, but sharpened with plenty of sportful malice', which 'was to be on the self conceit of "Mr Controller", otherwise Sir William Knollys (pronounced, and often written, Knowles) P.C., M.P., Comptroller of her Majesty's Household' (Hotson 1954, p. 99), this jest all with the permission of Lord Hunsdon, Lord Chamberlain of Elizabeth's Household. Hotson's case rests on a meticulous argument he mounts concerning the very first performance, or first night, of *Twelfth Night*.

In performances of *Twelfth Night*, Malvolio has always captured the audience's attention. The only surviving reference to the play being performed during Shakespeare's life is in the diary of John Manningham, a law student at the Middle Temple in London, who recorded the following on 2 February 1602:

At our feast we had a play called *Twelfth Night, or What You Will*, much like *The Comedy of Errors* or *Menaechmi* in

Plautus, but most like and near to that in Italian called
Inganni. A good practice in it to make the steward believe his
lady widow was in love with him, by counterfeiting a letter as
from his lady, in general terms telling him what she liked best
in him, and prescribing his gesture in smiling, his apparel, etc.,
and then when he came to practise, making him believe they
took him to be mad. (Schoenbaum 1975, p. 156)

It is remarkable that Manningham only mentions the Malvolio
plot. He mistakenly thinks Olivia is a widow, and mentions no
other characters at all. The forged-letter plot against Malvolio is
described as 'a good practice'. We are also provided with an
interesting insight into the knowledge Manningham has of some
of the sources of Shakespeare's play. But why does Malvolio
capture the attention so much when the play is performed? It
must be his outlandishness and ridiculousness when Maria's
device is fully working on him that makes him stick in the
memory of any who watch the play. As Maria says, when she is
encouraging Sir Toby and Fabian to come and see the absurd
figure of the once prim and proper steward behaving like a
smiling imbecile: 'If you desire the spleen, and will laugh yourselves in stitches, follow me' (3.2.63–4). The spleen was believed
to be the seat of laughter. With Sir Toby we say, 'Come bring us,
bring us where he is' (3.2.78), and we do follow Maria, along with
Sir Toby and Fabian. We all want a laugh, and if it is at someone
else's expense that does not generally prevent us from enjoying
ourselves. This is what makes *Twelfth Night* such an achievement
in comedy, for we take our laughter uproariously, we take our
comic pleasure, and then we start to sicken at the joke, we start
to wish it would end, we tire, we feel exhausted with the effort of
being amused by those on stage who are exhausted with the joke
themselves and we feel, surprisingly, pity for Malvolio. Aristotle
wrote:

Comedy represents the worse types of men; worse, however,
not in the sense that it embraces any and every kind of
badness, but in the sense that the ridiculous is a species of ugliness or badness. For the ridiculous consists in some form of

error or ugliness that is not painful or injurious; the comic mask, for example, is distorted and ugly, but causes no pain. (Aristotle 1965, p. 37)

In Shakespeare's comedy, however, there is pain. Why? Perhaps Shakespeare was aware that much laughter is a laughing *at* rather than a laughing *with*. The joke is often at someone's expense. Humour is often inherently cruel, and often ambiguous; it leaves us wondering about our ethics and morality.

Nigel Hawthorne is brilliantly cast in the role of Malvolio in Trevor Nunn's 1996 film version. Hawthorne, who is most famous for his role as 'Sir Humphrey' in the BBC satirical comedy *Yes Minister*, about British Government in the 1980s and early 1990s, portrays Malvolio as a busy head butler in Olivia's Edwardian mansion. His fingernail-inspecting, bespectacled disapproval of the efforts of the numerous kitchen staff forms an immediate and strong impression of priggish self-love and self-aggrandisement. We see him interrupted by the riotous behaviour of Sir Toby as he is reading *Amour* magazine. Hawthorne handles the madness of Malvolio capably, so it is ridiculous and disturbing at the same time. His most real moment is his closing ominous threat: 'I'll be revenged on the whole pack of you' (5.1.368). Here Hawthorne achieves tragic presence, and the play's content and contrived resolution wobbles and veers off kilter.

CHAPTER 8

ANTONIO AND SEBASTIAN

Our first impressions of Antonio and Sebastian as we read or see Act 2 Scene 1 are somewhat dependent on how much we want to read into their lines. What seems undeniable is that there is an inequality in the intensity of feeling here, and that if we were able to weigh emotion toward another in a set of scales then Antonio's pan would be the heavier. Sebastian seems desirous of departure from Antonio, whereas Antonio's desire is focused fully on Sebastian. We join the conversation, which we are led to believe has not just begun, with Antonio's heartfelt, 'Will you stay no longer, nor will you not that I go with you?' (2.1.1–2). But Antonio wants to be alone and, as politely as possible, tries to extract himself from a friendship he seems to find cloying. Antonio is insistent and, though Sebastian will not stay nor allow Antonio to accompany him, Antonio hopes he will at least be told where he is going. However, Sebastian remains aloof; though he does now reveal his identity to Antonio there is, it seems, a little bitterness in his account of his rescue:

No, sooth, sir. My determinate voyage is mere extravagancy. But I perceive in you so excellent a touch of modesty that you will not extort from me what I am willing to keep in. Therefore it charges me in manners the rather to express myself. You must know of me then, Antonio, my name is Sebastian, which I called Roderigo. My father was that Sebastian of Messaline whom I know you have heard of. He left behind him myself and a sister, both born in an hour. If the heavens had been pleased, would we had so ended. But you, sir, altered that, for some hour before you took me from the breach of the sea was my sister drowned. (2.1.9–20)

The depth of Antonio's feelings for Sebastian emerge with his plea, 'If you will not murder me for my love, let me be your servant' (2.1.31), but Sebastian is determined to part from him and leaves. Antonio at first feels that he cannot follow him to Orsino's court (Sebastian has, we note, perhaps as a final kindness to Antonio, indicated his planned destination) for he has 'many enemies' (2.1.40) there; however, his emotion gets the better of his judgement, feeling conquers reason, and he decides to risk his very life for his love: 'But come what may, I do adore thee so / That danger shall seem sport, and I will go' (2.1.42–3). As the Oxford editors point out, 'The relationship between Antonio and Sebastian is another of the differing "kinds of love" depicted in the play; but Shakespeare has dramatized it in a way that makes it hard to focus precisely' (Warren, p. 39).

Joseph Pequigney boldly attempts to '*secure* the homoerotic character of the friendship' between Antonio and Sebastian:

> . . . for months [Sebastian] has continuously remained with an adoring older man who is frankly desirous of him, who showered him with 'kindnesses' [3.4.341] and who, moreover, saved him from death at sea and nursed him back to health. It is the classic homoerotic relationship, wherein the mature lover serves as guide and mentor to the young beloved. (Warren, pp. 41–2)

On the use of the alias 'Roderigo' by Sebastian, Pequigney comments that it can be 'seen as a means to hide his identity, his true name and family connections, during a drawn-out sexual liaison with a stranger in strange lands' (Warren, p. 42). This seems an example of pushing character analysis too far; tempting as it is to 'fill in' gaps in our knowledge we must acknowledge other, more mundane possibilities. The audience needs to know who is speaking, and Sebastian's revelation of his true name to Antonio furnishes us with this vital information, information without which we would be in considerable confusion as to what was going on. The identification of this new arrival on the stage as Viola's 'lost' brother relaxes us in the confidence of a concordant comic resolution of the awkward predicament of lovers we have seen set in play. Then again, the evident desire of Antonio for Sebastian signals an intention on Shakespeare's part to complicate and make more knotty the situation at the very moment of suggesting a means of untying it.

We are presented with another scene (3.3) between Antonio and Sebastian which does nothing to allay our suspicions that theirs is a relationship of unequal strength of feeling. The scene begins with Sebastian's 'I would not by my will have troubled you, / But since you make your pleasure of your pains / I will no further chide you' (3.3.1–3). Again we sense a reticence on Sebastian's part, and when we compare his cool language with Antonio's passion the emotional imbalance is clearer:

> I could not stay behind you. My desire,
> More sharp than filèd steel, did spur me forth,
> And not all love to see you – though so much
> As might have drawn one to a longer voyage –
> But jealousy what might befall your travel,
> Being skilless in these parts, which to a stranger,
> Unguided and unfriended, often prove
> Rough and unhospitable. My willing love
> The rather by these arguments of fear
> Set forth in your pursuit. (3.3.4–13)

The startling image of Antonio's sharper-than-a-sword desire spurring him on in 'pursuit' of the younger man has been commented on by Valerie Traub, who argues that 'Antonio's discourse partakes of what I will call a "rhetoric of penetration".' (McDonald 2004, p. 716). In elaborating her point she claims:

> *Twelfth Night* represents male homoerotic desire as phallic in the most active sense: erect, hard, penetrating. Antonio describes his desire in terms of sharp, filed steel which spurs him on to pursuit, 'spur' working simultaneously to 'prick'

him (as object) and urge him on (as subject). (McDonald 2004, p. 716)

Antonio's declarations of 'desire', 'jealousy' and 'willing love' here fail to be reciprocated by Sebastian, who replies awkwardly, ending with a suggestion: 'What's to do? / Shall we go see the relics of this town' (3.3.18–19). But Antonio seems to have other ideas: 'Tomorrow sir, best first go see your lodging' (3.3.20). Antonio is forward here, and Sebastian's reply somewhat evasive: 'I am not weary, and 'tis long to night' (3.3.21); and he again suggests that they do a little sightseeing. Antonio is fearful of capture as he has a reputation in Illyria as a bloody pirate, and Sebastian seizes on this knowledge to suggest that he conceal himself: 'Do not then walk too open' (3.3.37). Does Sebastian quite like the idea of leaving Antonio behind again? If so he is to be disappointed, for his insistent pursuer then gives him his purse and tells him where to lodge, and that he will order their meal and meet him there later. His final line seems unequivocally hopeful of a sexual liaison: 'There shall you have me' (3.3.42). Furthermore, when Sebastian asks why he has been given Antonio's purse, Antonio replies to the slightly bewildered Sebastian: 'Haply your eye shall light upon some toy / You have desire to purchase; and your store / I think is not for idle markets, sir' (3.3.44–6). This encouragement to Sebastian to indulge his desire with frivolous spending seems to be more about Antonio's desire. Could we say that he is grooming the younger man for the evening he hopes lies ahead? Olivia's third line in the following scene certainly adds to this impression of Antonio as predatory and corrupting: 'For youth is bought more oft than begged or borrowed' (3.4.3).

When, later in Act 3 Scene 4, Antonio mistakes Viola for Sebastian, we see the comedy of the duel between Aguecheek and Cesario replaced by Antonio's 'outburst of intense suffering, and a public declaration of his love for Sebastian' (Warren, p. 40):

Let me speak a little. This youth that you see here
I snatched one half out of the jaws of death,
Relieved him with such sanctity of love,

And to his image, which methought did promise
Most venerable worth, did I devotion. (3.4.350–4)

This is one of the remarkable aspects of *Twelfth Night*: that the
mood can switch so dramatically and convincingly. Antonio's
mention of Sebastian feeds Viola's imagination and gives her
hope that he lives. The slapstick humour of the absurd mock
combat is all but forgotten as we enter the final phase of the play,
a phase in which the atmosphere is extremely fraught and the
characters' emotions are running high.

Antonio's desire makes him a more interesting character than
Viola's identical twin, Sebastian, who seems to move through the
play in a kind of dream. Shakespeare gives Antonio a long
speech to Orsino in the play's final scene, a speech designed as an
outpouring of emotion from a most unlikely source, a 'notable
pirate' and 'salt-water thief' (5.1.63), as Orsino brands him
(names which he denies):

A witchcraft drew me hither:
That most ingrateful boy there by your side
From the rude sea's enraged and foamy mouth
Did I redeem. A wreck past hope he was.
His life I gave him, and did thereto add
My love without retention or restraint,
All his in dedication. For his sake
Did I expose myself, pure for his love,
Into the danger of this adverse town,
Drew to defend him when he was beset,
Where being apprehended, his false cunning –
Not meaning to partake with me in danger –
Taught him to face me out of his acquaintance,
And grew a twenty years' removèd thing
While one would wink, denied me mine own purse,
Which I had recommended to his use
Not half an hour before. (5.1.70–86)

In his answer to Orsino's enquiry as to when Viola/Sebastian
came to this town Antonio reveals what is perhaps the most

suggestive evidence of their sexual liaison when he claims that for 'three months before, / No int'rim, not a minute's vacancy, / Both day and night did we keep company' (5.1.89–91). Perhaps the desire is not so one-sided as was earlier suggested, for when Sebastian later sees Antonio his words are indeed passionate: 'Antonio! O my dear Antonio, / How have the hours racked and tortured me / Since I have lost thee!' (5.1.211–13). This seems to add weight to Pequigney's interpretation and invites an agreement with Warren and Wells:

> even if the arguments put forward by Pequigney and others do not 'secure' the Antonio/Sebastian relationship as homoerotic, it is certainly true that the text permits, even if it does not demand, a homoerotic interpretation. (Warren, p. 42)

But, for all this intensity of emotion and perhaps mutual erotic attraction between Sebastian and Antonio, the play ends with Sebastian reunited with his sister, married to Olivia and seemingly content. Antonio's desire for Sebastian, sharp as it may be, seems to have no point to it. He has been spurred on in pursuit of the young man and risked his very life in that pursuit, but his final lines subsume him in the general sense of wonder as he comments on the likeness of the twins, no longer certain of the identity of the man he loves: 'How have you made division of yourself? / An apple cleft in two is not more twin / Than these two creatures. Which is Sebastian?' (5.1.216–18). When Olivia declares 'Most wonderful!' (5.1.219) she may be seen to speak generally for those on and off stage, expressing a sense of miraculous joy. But for Antonio, we feel, there is no joy in the wonder, more a sense of perplexity and loss as he ends the play with no hope of fulfilment of his sharp desire.

THROUGH THE CHARACTERS TO THE KEY THEMES AND ISSUES

COMEDY AND CARNIVAL

John Draper's character-based approach leads him to conclude that Shakespeare has created more than just stock figures of the traditional comedy, but rather complex characters that approximate real life: 'So drama, in its reactions of plot and character, expresses in human terms the eternal interaction of relativity: and surely no comedy does so with more brilliance and more delicacy than does *Twelfth Night*' (Draper 1950, p. 230). But the purpose of this book, while encouraging a close consideration and appreciation of Shakespeare's complex characters, is to make readers careful not to be swept up in this sort of enthusiasm for Shakespeare's achievement to the point where they fail to see characters as the fictional constructs, the products of feigning poetry, the illusion created by the marks on a page (characters of another sort; see Chapter One) that they are. It is hard to avoid this error, for in his plays Shakespeare repeatedly conjures what seem like real people into being.

Consideration of the characters of *Twelfth Night* inescapably leads us beyond character into themes and issues. Thinking about Feste, Sir Toby Belch, Aguecheek and Malvolio particularly, we cannot avoid thinking about the kind of comedy Shakespeare has concocted. Belch and Malvolio seem to represent more than individuals who disagree with each other. Shakespeare positions Belch quite clearly as a Lord of Misrule with swollen belly, a sure sign of his huge appetite for food and drink in a time of carnival, and Malvolio as the puritanical voice of disapproval attempting to restrain these carnivalistic energies. The opposition of these two characters and principles of life is most clearly dramatized in Act 2 Scene 3 of the play when Malvolio disturbs their midnight rioting (a scene discussed earlier in Chapter Seven). Malvolio seems here to stand for Lenten abstemiousness (even today some still give up something for Lent) while Toby is the embodiment of carnivalesque misrule. His famous attack on Malvolio captures the essence of the dispute between festival-lovers and rising puritan forces in English Elizabethan society: 'Art any more than a steward? Dost thou think because thou art virtuous there shall be no more cakes and ale?' (2.3.106–8). These are questions that strike at Malvolio's rank and his priggish conviction of his superiority to those less continent than himself. Warren and Wells point out in their note on 'cakes and ale' that these pleasures were 'associated with church festivals, and so abhorrent to a puritan, as would be the reference in the next line to Saint Anne, mother of the Virgin Mary' (Warren, p. 129). The next line, a most puzzling one for the modern reader, is Feste's: 'Yes, by Saint Anne, and ginger shall be hot i'th' mouth too' (2.3.109), which becomes clearer as an attack on puritan restraint when we read in the note that ginger was 'used to spice ale, and regarded as an aphrodisiac' (Warren, p. 130). Feste is supporting Belch's attack on Malvolio, and introducing a notion of sexual liberty resulting from the excesses of drinking.

Why is the attack on Malvolio so strong, and why are so many characters (Sir Toby, Feste, Maria, Sir Andrew, Fabian) involved in it? The puritan forces with which Malvolio is connected in the play, both implicitly and explicitly, were very real in Elizabethan England. The following extract is taken from a 1579 publication by a young poet and playwright turned puritan, Stephen Gosson, entitled *The Schoole of Abuse, Containing a pleasaunt invective against Poets, Pipers, Plaiers, Jesters and such like Caterpillers of a Commonwealth*:

They that lack customers all the week, either because their haunt is unknown, or the constables and officers of the parish watch them so narrowly that they dare not quetch, to celebrate the Sabbath flock to theatres, and there keep a general market of bawdry. Not that any filthiness in deed is committed within the compass of that ground, as was done in Rome, but that every wanton and his paramour, every man and his mistress, every John and his Joan, every knave and his quean, are there first acquainted and cheapen the merchandise in that place, which they pay for elsewhere as they can agree. (Evans 1987, p. 20)

'Quetch' here means 'stir', while 'quean' means 'harlot, strumpet' (*OED*). Gosson's view of the theatre as 'a general market of bawdry' was one generally held by puritans, who attacked plays and theatres not just for the immorality of the audience but also for the immorality of the plays themselves and the actors who played in them. Boys dressing up as women was a favourite target for puritan critics. Comedies, in their release of transgressive sexual energies, were seen as particularly corrupting. On 28 July 1597 an official letter was sent from the Lord Mayor of London and the Aldermen to the Privy Council containing the following complaints about 'the inconveniences that grow by stage-plays about the City of London':

They are a special cause of corrupting their youth, containing nothing but unchaste matters, lascivious desires, shifts of cozenage, and other lewd and ungodly practices, being so as that they impress the very quality and corruption of manners which they represent, contrary to the rules and art prescribed for the making of comedies even among the heathen, who used them seldom and at certain set times, and not all the year long as our manner is. Whereby such as frequent them, being of the base and refuse sort of people, or such young gentlemen as have small regard of credit or conscience, draw the same into imitation and not to the avoiding the like vices which they represent. (Evans 1987, pp. 5–6)

Of special interest to us here is the reference to the 'making of comedies'. The problem is perceived to be that the comedies are performed 'all the year long' and not 'seldom and at certain set times' as they were 'even among the heathen'. In 1590s London there was an increasing population who wanted entertainment, and there was money to be made from comedies like Shakespeare's *Twelfth Night*, not just during certain festive periods, but all year round.

The theatres were defended against the puritans by the Queen herself, the Court, the Privy Council, the humanists and, of course, the playwrights and actors like Shakespeare. In *Twelfth Night* even the idiotic Sir Andrew Aguecheek makes an abusive reference to the puritans when he says to Sir Toby, 'policy I hate. I had as lief be a Brownist as a politician' (3.2.29) ('lief' meaning rather). A 'Brownist' was a 'member of an extreme puritan sect founded in 1581 by Robert Browne (c.1550–1633) who advocated the separation of church and state' (Warren, p. 164). The portrayal of a figure such as Malvolio can be seen as a somewhat satirical attack on the anti-theatrical puritan forces at work in Elizabethan society. Malvolio is linked with the puritans in a number of ways other than directly being labelled 'a kind of puritan', as he is by Maria. For example, in his soliloquy at 3.4.62–80, discussed in Chapter Seven, Malvolio says that 'no dram of a scruple, no scruple of a scruple, no obstacle, no incredulous or unsafe circumstance [. . .] can come between me and the full prospect of my hopes' (3.4.75–9). Warren and Wells comment that this speech 'brilliantly brings out the logic of Malvolio's thinking' and that it is, perhaps, an example of his 'puritan precision, for another contemporary name for puritan was "precisian", "one who is rigidly precise or punctilious in the observance of rules or forms" (*OED*, *precisian*)' (Warren, p. 173). One of the characteristics of Shakespeare's portrayal of Malvolio as a 'kind of puritan' is the steward's disapproval of bear-baiting, a rival entertainment to the theatres (the Bear Garden, where bear-baiting and bull-baiting took place, was situated near the Globe Theatre on the south bank of the Thames). Malvolio may have brought Fabian 'out o' favour with my lady about a bear-baiting' (2.5.6–7) in the past, but now he will become the bear. In having the 'pack' of characters (Maria, Belch, Aguecheek, Fabian and Feste) 'baiting' the priggish steward, Shakespeare demonstrates a canny understanding of his audience's taste for blood in their entertainment (but perhaps wants them to question it). Another linkage of Malvolio with the puritans is Sir Toby's reference to him as a 'niggardly rascally sheep-biter' (2.5.4–5). The term 'sheep-biter' was used in the Elizabethan period as a way of describing a 'hypocritical puritan' as it refers to a dog that attacks sheep and was used to denote a man who, while appearing virtuous and godly, is actually a 'whore-monger' (Warren, p. 141).

It was the brilliant Russian critic, Mikhail Bakhtin, in his book *Rabelais and His World* (first published in English in 1968), who invented the term 'carnivalesque', a term which he describes in the following way:

> The temporary suspension, both ideal and real, of hierarchical rank created during carnival time a special type of communication impossible in everyday life. This led to the creation of special forms of marketplace speech and gesture, frank and free, permitting no distance between those who came in contact with each other and liberating from norms of etiquette and decency imposed at other times [. . .]We find here a characteristic logic, the peculiar logic of the 'inside out', of the 'turnabout', of a continual shifting from top to bottom, from front to rear, of numerous parodies and travesties, humiliations, profanations, comic crownings and uncrownings. A second life, a second world of folk culture is thus constructed; it is to a certain extent a parody of the extracarnival [i.e. of the normal world outside the carnival], a 'world inside out'. (Rivkin and Ryan 1998, p. 46)

We can see the world turned upside down and inside out in *Twelfth Night* in many moments, such as the sexual innuendo between Maria and Aguecheek in Act 1 Scene 3, the erotic interplay of gender and sexuality between Olivia and Viola in Act 1 Scene 5 and the entirety of the trick played on Malvolio in which he is subverted (by inferiors such as Maria and Fabian) by being encouraged in his over-reaching fantasies of marrying Olivia, a Countess who is clearly his superior and therefore out of his sphere. The gulling of Malvolio also involves other forms of subversion, in particular of Olivia's rule of her household, for Maria forges her mistress's handwriting and Maria, Toby, Fabian and Feste knowingly abuse the steward of her household, preventing him from fulfilling his proper responsibilities.

In terms of relating the play to traditional festivities in early-modern England, C. L. Barber has prepared the ground nicely for modern scholars with his study of *Shakespeare's Festive Comedy* (1959). His book is 'an exploration of the way the social form of Elizabethan holidays contributed to the dramatic form of festive comedy' and his intention 'to relate this drama to holiday has', he claims, 'proved to be the most effective way to describe its character' (Barber 1959, p. 4). As an exploration of the variety of Elizabethan festival customs and how they relate to Shakespeare's comedy generally, Barber's book is instructive, and when he turns to *Twelfth Night* in particular he makes insightful remarks on the play's title; the preponderance of delusion and misapprehension in the play ('*Madness* is a key word' (p. 242)); the folly of misrule; and the play's proximity to other, seemingly more problematic plays, such as *Hamlet*, *Troilus and Cressida*, *Measure for Measure* and *All's Well That Ends Well*. In the case of the last two plays Barber suggests that 'it is quite possible' that they 'did not seem to Shakespeare and his audiences so different from *Twelfth Night* as they seem to us' (p. 258). Barber comments that Feste in particular 'has been over the garden wall into some such world as the Vienna of *Measure for Measure*' (a dark and strange place indeed), and that he 'has an air of knowing more of life than anyone else' which has the effect of 'suggesting that the whole bright revel emerges from shadow' (p. 259).

Modern critical responses to the play, and performances and film versions of the past few decades, have tended to bring out this shadow-side of the play. Billington's account of the performance history of the play quotes John Gielgud: 'It is so difficult to combine the romance of the play with the cruelty of the jokes against Malvolio, jokes which are in any case archaic and difficult. The different elements in the play are hard to balance properly' (Billington 1990, p. xvii). In Gielgud's 1955 production Billington remembers Laurence Olivier's Malvolio as 'camp' and feels that his performance 'was redeemed only by the whiplash fury he revealed in Malvolio's exit line which introduced a note of Lear-like revenge into Illyria' (p. xvii). It was in 1958 that Peter Hall directed a production of the play that 'solved many of the play's problems':

> Most directors of *Twelfth Night* see the play as made up of a romantic half and a comic half. Hall's genius was to see that these divisions were not watertight: that the romance was invaded by high-spirited fun and the comedy by a grave melancholy. (Billington 1990, p. xvii)

John Barton's 1969 production at Stratford, revived in 1971, was 'legendary', a critical success due to Barton's 'unremitting exploration of text and sub-text, his detailed exploration of character, and his well-nigh perfect achievement of the balance between comedy and tears' (Billington 1990, p. xxi). Terry Hands' 1979 production was 'full of the wild exuberance of young love', while John Caird's 1983 RSC revival 'was widely perceived to be dark, autumnal and melancholic' (p. xxvi). In 1987 Bill Alexander produced the play at Stratford-upon-Avon with Antony Sher in the role of Malvolio. Billington remarks that 'the intention here, quite clearly, was to push both the comedy and tragedy of Malvolio to its utmost limits' (p. xxviii). Trevor Nunn's 1996 film version was criticized by Kevin Jackson in *The Independent on Sunday* for its bleakness, with Jackson claiming that 'murk is drowning every frame'. Jackson is wrong, however, for Nunn's filmic rendering genuinely reflects the cruelty in the play's humour, the play's strong sense of loss in love and its recurring anxiety about ageing and death.

Readers must remember that the play is much more than an entertaining comedy featuring a group of memorable characters. *Twelfth Night* works, through the interplay of its characters, to raise questions concerning so many aspects of human life such as: the nature of love (in its various forms); judgement; power (or lack of it); class; money and giving; leisure and work; humour; desire; cruelty; disguise; excess and restraint; and time. The characters, interacting in the imagined space of Illyria, draw us beyond a response to them as individual people and into a consideration of these themes and issues, as the preceding chapters have demonstrated.

STAGING DESIRE AND CRUELTY

When we consider the possibilities for actual performance of the scene between Olivia and Viola in Act 1 Scene 5, or the scene between Viola and Orsino in Act 2 Scene 4, we are astounded by the complexity of the semiotics involved in such dramatic moments, and our complex and varying responses to such moments, as individual audience members, is suggestively captured by Valerie Traub in her essay 'Desire and the Difference it Makes':

> From the perspective of this counter-discourse, psychoanalysis reduces sexuality to one variable – object choice (whether 'latent' or manifest) – which is presumed to flow directly from gender identity. The contradiction at the heart of this problem, as well as the alternatives posed by this counter-discourse, can be better understood by imagining oneself in the following voyeuristic scenario: when viewing a love scene on a movie screen, you experience pleasure by watching an interplay of power and erotic desire. Your eye is drawn to particular body zones, and you are aroused not only by body type and position, but also by the 'scene', the pace of interaction, the affective content. But whether you are aroused by watching a woman's body or a man's, two women together or two men, a woman with a man, or any other combination imaginable, the mere fact of your excitement does not explain what is happening on the dual levels of identification and erotic desire. That is, is your arousal dependent upon a process of identification with or desire for an eroticised object? To state it simplistically, do you *want* or do you *want to be* one of the images on the screen? Which one? Can you tell? Does your identification and/or desire shift during the interaction? And are your desire and identification dependent upon the *gender* or any one of many other constituents of the image: power,

class, status, age, relative aggressivity, vulnerability, energy level, clothing, skin colour/texture, hair type/length, genital size/shape . . .? Do specific acts (sucking, penetration, kissing) seem more relevant to your identification and/or desire than the gender of persons involved? (Wayne 1991, p. 89)

To be sure, *Twelfth Night* and *As You Like It* work on audiences in complex ways. The heroines of these comedies, Viola and Rosalind, both disguise themselves as men, and by so doing they unleash all sorts of interesting sexual energies, both embodying in themselves and inviting in others, transgression of traditional gender behaviours and roles in their uncertain and unstable duality. On Shakespeare's stage this complex effect was heightened by the fact that boys or young men played the roles. By the end of each play there is a sense that the holiday period is coming to a close and, as we do on Twelfth Night, all the trinkets and paraphernalia of that festive time are put away until next year. Comedies end in marriages, and these marriages signal a return to 'normal' patterns of behaviour. As Catherine Belsey puts it:

Closure depends on closing off the glimpsed transgression and reinstating a clearly defined sexual difference. But the plays are more than their endings, and the heroines become wives only after they have been shown to be something altogether more singular – because more plural. (McDonald 2004, p. 647)

However, the mask of 'normality' has slipped, and as we leave the theatre we feel that the liberating, energizing effect of Shakespeare's comic play may not end with the play's end.

So much for the erotics of staging desire, but what of the sport of staging cruelty? The height of cruelty in the play must be the disturbing Act 4 Scene 2 in which Feste, disguised as Sir Topaz the curate, visits Malvolio in his cell of 'hideous darkness' (4.2.31). It is a scene that is difficult for us to judge as it seems so unpleasant and nasty to a twenty-first-century audience, a practical joke taken far too far. But would it have seemed so cruel to the Elizabethan audience, and should we allow it to overshadow the entire play? Shakespeare does seem here to be clearly indicating that the pleasure of the joke is waning, tipping over into something very far from pleasure, something sinister and wicked even. As the scene unfolds, even Sir Toby is tiring of the 'sport' and instructs the dissembling Feste to approach Malvolio again:

> To him in thine own voice, and bring me word how thou find'st him. I would we were well rid of this knavery. If he may be conveniently delivered, I would he were, for I am now so far in offence with my niece that I cannot pursue with any safety this sport to the upshot. Come by and by to my chamber. (4.2.66–71)

There are a few points which arise from this passage. The 'sport' to which Sir Toby refers here is the tormenting of Malvolio in a dark prison cell. Sir Toby is drained and well aware of the potential trouble he will be in with Olivia when she finds out what has been going on. To Olivia, we recall, Malvolio is a valued servant and she genuinely seems to care for (or at least need) him. When she witnesses Malvolio's bizarre behaviour in Act 3 Scene 4 she is distracted by thoughts of 'the young gentleman of the Count Orsino's' (3.4.54) who, a nameless servant informs her, 'attends your ladyship's pleasure' (3.4.56). She immediately replies, 'I'll come to him.' Nevertheless, Olivia then finds time to stress that her steward, suffering as she perceives him to be from 'very midsummer madness' (3.4.53), should be looked after: 'Good Maria, let this fellow be looked to. Where's my cousin Toby? Let some of my people have a special care of him, I would not have him miscarry for the half of my dowry' (3.4.58–61). In the light of this remark, Maria's and Toby's treatment of Malvolio seems particularly inexcusable, and a sign of disrespect and mockery of Olivia's express wishes.

Why do they torment Malvolio so? A bill or a poster used to advertise an event gives a good idea of what the Elizabethan 'sport' of bear-baiting involved:

> Tomorrowe beinge Thursdaie shalbe seen at the Beargardin on the banckside a greate mach plaid by the gamstirs of Essex who hath challenged all comers what soever to plaie v dogges

at the single bear for v pounds and also to wearie a bull dead at the stake and for your better content shall have plasant sport with the horse and ape and whipping of the blind beare. (Halliday 1964, p. 55)

Halliday explains that 'the whipping of the blind bear, Harry Hunks, "till the blood ran down his old shoulders" was a humorous interlude, as was also the baiting by dogs of a horse with an ape tied to its back' (p. 55). Thursdays were the day set aside for animal-baiting of this kind, and in 1591 a decree was passed by the Privy Council prohibiting plays at theatres on Thursdays, presumably to ensure no competition for the animal-baiters. The puritans vehemently opposed the practice of bear- and bull-baiting, attributing the collapse of scaffolds around the Bear Garden in 1583, which killed eight people, to the wrath of God. Baiting was prohibited by Parliament at the beginning of the Civil War (1642) but re-established with the Stuart Restoration (Halliday 1964, pp. 55–6).

The sport of bear-baiting is clearly referred to and alluded to in *Twelfth Night* in a number of places. When Fabian joins the pack of pranksters he informs Toby of his motive for wanting to see Malvolio 'come by some notable shame' (2.5.5): 'You know he brought me out o'favour with my lady about a bear-baiting here' (2.5.7). Sir Toby's reply wittily implies that by having 'the bear again' (presumably Malvolio himself) they will 'anger him' (Malvolio) 'and we will fool him black and blue, shall we not' (2.5.8–9), conflating Malvolio and the bear in an image of physical cruelty (the black and blue of bruising). Maria's earlier parting shot to Malvolio, when he attempted to prevent the riotous midnight partying of Sir Toby, Sir Andrew and Feste, was to say, 'Go shake your ears' (2.3.116). It is an odd expression and so, as discussed in Chapter Seven, we turn to the notes for edification. Warren and Wells tell us that 'Stephen Dickey ('Shakespeare's Mastiff Comedy', *SQ* 42 (1991), 255–75) sees the phrase as one of several allusions to bear-baiting in the play'. Dickey quotes from Robert Langham's account of the 'Princely Pleasures' at Kenilworth Castle in 1575 'where a baited bear is said to "shake his ears twice or thrice with the blood and the slaver about his physiognomy" ' (Warren, p. 130). So Maria's 'Go shake your ears' may be alluding to bloody bear-baiting practices, a possible counter-threat to dismiss Malvolio, who has just been threatening her with telling Olivia about her giving 'means' (wine in this case) 'for this uncivil rule' (2.3.115). Olivia surprisingly uses an image from bear-baiting herself when she describes the effect that Cesario is having upon her: 'Have you not set mine honour at the stake / And baited it with all th'unmuzzled thoughts / That tyrannous heart can think' (3.1.116–18; this passage has been discussed in Chapter Six). Fabian mentions that Viola, in fear of Aguecheek, 'pants and looks pale as if a bear were at his heels' (3.4.283). But the clearest and most significant allusion to bear-baiting comes in Malvolio's final line: 'I'll be revenged on the whole pack of you' (5.1.368).

Given the link established between Malvolio and puritanism and the puritans' hatred of bear-baiting and the theatre, it seems irresistible not to think of Malvolio's final line both as an image of the cruel baiting he has suffered as the slavering pack came at him from all angles, and as Shakespeare's prophecy of the puritan backlash against these unrestrained, year-round, carnivalesque, festive, drunken, bawdy energies. And powerful and accurate prophecy it appears to be, for Malvolio's puritanical revenge will encompass the whole pack of them: the jester Feste; the drunken dissolute Sir Toby; the diminutive Lady of Misrule Maria; the foolish gull Sir Andrew and the bear-baiting Fabian. All will be punished in the England that is coming, an England in which the snowballing puritan forces would close the theatres and ban bear-baiting (and even ban Christmas, the festive period celebrated in *Twelfth Night*) in 1642, the year of the English Revolution and the beginning of the Civil War. The two sides in that war seem already at each other's throats in Shakespeare's *Twelfth Night*.

LANGUAGE

Cruelty and erotic play are not, of course, only physical. Both can work very effectively through the spoken or written word. Flirtation is a good example, as here between Sebastian and Olivia:

Sebastian: What relish is in this? How runs the stream?
Or I am mad, or else this is a dream.
Let fancy still my sense in Lethe steep.
If it be thus to dream, still let me sleep.
Olivia: Nay, come, I prithee, would thou'dst be ruled by me.
Sebastian: Madam, I will.
Olivia: O, say so, and so be. (4.1.58–63)

One can feel the passion bristling and crackling. Olivia will rule
Sebastian's heart. Her heart, started, frightened by Toby's rude
skirmishing with Sebastian/Cesario, is overwhelmed with joy at
his surrender. Her final line here before they exit is a rapturous
'O, say so, and so be', and how lascivious might the line be in
performance, how full of manifest desire? This section will illus-
trate the way in which Shakespeare's specific language often
requires us to think about the place and the time that these extraordinary play-texts were created. Without such contemplation
and research into the culture of Elizabethan England we are in
danger of incomprehension or misapprehension and this necessarily takes us beyond characters and characterization into questions of textuality and history. The play is about language itself
and contains so much wordplay that it can leave the modern
reader's mind reeling. Consider Antonio's speech to Sebastian in
Act 3 Scene 3:

Antonio: Hold sir, here's my purse,
In the south suburbs at the Elephant
Is best to lodge. I will bespeak our diet
Whiles you beguile the time and feed your knowledge
With viewing of the town. There shall you have me. (3.3.38–42)

A few lines further on Antonio reminds Sebastian of the place to
meet him: 'To th'Elephant', to which Sebastian replies, 'I do
remember' (3.3.48). This is an early-modern example of 'product
placement', that device by which those who work in the modern
media advertise products surreptitiously (and not so surreptitiously). The Elephant was a pub which Shakespeare and his
audience knew well, on the south bank of the Thames in Elephant

Alley, very close to the Globe Theatre (Donno 1985, p. 107). Gustav Ungerer held that it was 'an inn-cum-brothel' (Warren, p. 168). But what is it doing in Illyria? And why does Antonio mention it twice? In typical style Shakespeare seems to be killing two birds with one stone, developing the sense of Antonio's insistent, even obsessive, pursuit of Sebastian, but also advertising a nearby hostelry where, no doubt, Shakespeare himself drank and enjoyed himself. Here we are offering an explanation of the play's 'Elephant' reference by thinking of the material culture in which the play was originally produced. Shakespeare uses 'the Elephant' because it is part of his world. But it is not part of our world, so we need to work to recover its meaning.

Twelfth Night is a play which abounds in topical references which puzzle the reader and which present particular difficulties for those performing the play and wanting it to be comprehended and enjoyed by their audiences. John Caird says there are 'major problems' in Act 3 Scenes 2 and 4 due to the large number of 'dead jokes' and the disruption in the play's rhythm caused by the fact that 'Belch goes on and on' (Billington 1990, pp. 21–2). One can see his point when reading these scenes, for they do contain many terms which are lost on us, unless we have the assistance of a helpful editor. When Sir Toby is encouraging Sir Andrew to challenge Viola to a fencing duel he says:

> Taunt him with the licence of ink. If thou 'thou'st' him some thrice, it shall not be amiss, and as many lies as will lie in thy sheet of paper, although the sheet were big enough for the bed of Ware in England, set 'em down, go about it. (3.2.41–5)

What, we ask ourselves, is 'the bed of Ware'? Without specifically knowing we understand enough to see that Toby is punning on 'sheet' (of paper, for a bed) and 'lie' (tell untruths, lie down) here. His mention of England reminds the audience of the fiction that the action is taking place in Illyria at the same time as reminding them that they are in England. How helpful, then, is it to know that the bed of Ware is 'a famous large carved-oak bedstead 10 feet 9 inches square, now in the Victoria and Albert Museum, London' (Lothian and Craik 1975, p. 86), or that it was 'famous among the Elizabethans [. . .] and could accommodate a dozen people' (Donno 1985, p. 104)? The extra information we are furnished with by Lothian and Donno does help us to appreciate how Sir Toby's mention of the bed of Ware, a giant bed even by today's standards, would have added a sense of outlandish exaggeration, fitting for Toby's larger-than-life character, to his encouragement of Sir Andrew.

In discussing the problems of these topical references for directors and performers of the play, Michael Billington asks, 'What do you do about lines' like Sir Toby's 'Are they like to take dust, like Mistress Mall's picture' (1.3.119) or Malvolio's 'The Lady of the Strachey married the yeoman of the wardrobe' (2.5.36)? Bill Alexander argues that some references, such as the reference to Mistress Mall, are so topical that they are 'probably utterly unintelligible' while others, such as Malvolio's about the lady and the yeoman, have 'a universal comprehensibility' (Billington 1990, p. 20). Malvolio's reference to the lady and the yeoman is clearly about class difference and expresses his aspiration to marry Olivia. We can understand the sense of this in performance. But what of Mistress Mall's picture? More information about this reference might be of interest, and so we turn again to textual editors and commentators for edification. If we look at the Cambridge edition notes we read that 'Mall is a diminutive of Mary, perhaps used here generically, perhaps in reference to Maria' (Donno 1985, p. 55). Donno's comment seems to go nowhere, so we turn to the Arden edition where we find the following: 'Various Marys have been put forward: Mary Frith alias Moll Cutpurse (Steevens), Mary Ambree (Barnett), Mary Carlton (Grey) (for details see Furness), Moll Newberry (Wilson), Mary Fitton (Hotson), Maria in this play (Luce)' (Lothian and Craik 1975, pp. 17–18). This is more helpful and gives us various options for further research. But which route should we follow? When we turn to the Oxford edition we find the note to Mistress Mall's picture reads: 'Mall, like Moll, was a nickname for Mary. Various Malls have been suggested for this allusion (if it is one). The likeliest is Mary Fitton, one of Elizabeth I's maids of honour, disgraced for bearing the Earl of Pembroke's child in 1601 (see Hotson, pp. 103–6)' (Warren, p. 99). So we turn to Hotson for more information and find an account of the whole affair from which the following serves as a taste:

> In 1595 the lovely Mall Fitton was admitted at the age of seventeen as one of the royal Cynthia's Maids of Honour – the band of Court 'glories' dressed all in chaste and virgin white, with whom 'all things must be not only without lust, but without suspicion of lightness' [. . .] A few months before Shakespeare's *Twelfth Night*, the twenty-two-year-old beauty, then high in favour with the Queen, involved herself with William Lord Herbert, afterwards Earl of Pembroke – who has been fancied as Shakespeare's 'W. H.' [to whom the sonnets are dedicated. Hotson's account tells of Mary Fitton becoming pregnant by William Herbert, thus bringing scandal on Elizabeth's court] Besmirching shame lay in wait for her all-admired face. She had therefore withdrawn it, like a curtained picture, from the vulgar gaze, providing Shakespeare's Sir Toby Belch with his passing allusion – 'Wherefore are these things hid? . . . Are they like to take dust, like Mistress Mal's picture?' Before the end of January, the very month of Twelfth Night, she was committed to custody. (Hotson 1954, pp. 103–6)

Hotson's explanation allows him a further speculation into the true meaning of Malvolio's name. He argues that Olivia's steward, as a parody of Sir William Knollys, Controller of Elizabeth's household, has a name which alludes to his infatuation with the said Mary Fitton, a much younger woman in his trust. The name Malvolio exposes not only the 'ill-will' of Knollys but 'also deftly fetches up Knollys' ridiculous love-chase of Mistress Mall by a slight modulation of *Malavoglia* into '*Mal'-voglio* – which means "I want Mall", "I wish for Mall", "I will have Mall". It is a masterpiece of mockery' (Hotson 1954, p. 108).

And so we have followed the trail, from Shakespeare's writing of Sir Toby's words 'Mistress Mall's picture', into history. The name may be randomly selected, but more likely it means something, and our research demonstrates the possibility of exploring that meaning in relation to the rest of the play, Shakespeare's

Elizabethan London culture, a story of the sexual liberty of Elizabeth's maid of honour Mistress Mall Fitton and the ultimate restraint of her incarceration. It may not be a world to hide virtues in, but when vice is seen there is much shame that follows in its wake.

TIME

Feste tells us in his song that 'A great while ago the world begun' (5.1.395). It seems, as much as any line in the play, to be an expression of timeless truth, understandable in any place – now, then or to come – requiring no elucidation. However, Hotson states that 'Feste's "A great while ago the world begun" recalls the Elizabethan euphemism for coition, "To dance The Beginning of the World"' (Hotson 1954, p. 171). It is a fascinating example of how, as scholars of literature, we can take nothing for granted. Language is part of a whole structure of signs that change with history.

Shakespeare writes so much about time that it is difficult to know where to look for suggestive links between Feste's reference to the beginning of the world and his trail through a human life – seeming to evoke thoughts of the universal cosmic sense of time, from creation to doomsday, beginning to end, mirroring the particular individual span of years from birth to death. Feste's final song is echoed in *King Lear*, where Lear's fool sings a further verse:

> He that has and a little tiny wit,
>> With hey, ho, the wind and the rain,
> Must make content with his fortunes fit,
>> Though the rain it raineth every day. (*King Lear* 3.2.73–6)

Lear's fool keeps the second and fourth lines of Feste's stanzas, reminding us again of the unavoidable sense of time's melancholy progress and the relentless fact of rain, rain, rain.

There is another echo, of Feste's concluding stanza and of Lear's fall from kingship to beggary, in *All's Well That Ends Well*. The King ends that play with a similar reminder to Feste's of the effort of the theatrical enterprise in which William Shakespeare, Robert Armin (who most likely played Feste and Lear's fool) and their fellow actors are involved:

> The king's a beggar now the play is done.
> All is well ended if this suit be won.
> That you express content, which we will pay
> With strife to please you, day exceeding day.
> Ours be your patience, and yours our parts,
> Your gentle hands lend us, and take our hearts. (*All's Well* 5.3.358–63)

These links to Shakespeare's other plays remind us of themes that are larger than individual characters. And with any consideration of Shakespeare's presentation of time in his plays the extraordinary sonnet cycle should also be included. The vital importance of perceptions of social and sexual difference and how individuals might love across the boundaries these differences present is explored in the 154 sonnets of Shakespeare's sequence and fascinating links can be made between these sonnets and *Twelfth Night*. In his stimulating article 'Love and Service in *Twelfth Night* and the Sonnets', David Schalkwyk writes:

> Love has all but vanished from current critical discourse. Since the theoretical transformation of Shakespeare studies some twenty years ago, scholars have been reluctant to engage with either the word or the concept in Shakespeare's work. A pair of terms that now regularly do service in its place – *power* and *desire* – have replaced *love*. The word is impossibly general and vague, while power and desire, properly theorized, have promised to strip love of its murkiness and sentimentality. (Schalkwyk 2005, p. 76)

Schalkwyk claims that '*Twelfth Night* is as much a study of service and master-servant relations as it is a comedy of romantic love' (p. 86) and goes on to describe how closely implicated the idea of 'service' is in so many of the relationships between characters in the play:

Every instance of desire in the play is intertwined with service: Viola's status as Orsino's servant is the condition of possibility and impossibility of her love for him and also of Olivia's erotic desire for her as Cesario; Orsino himself embodies courtly infatuation as a form of service in his dotage on Olivia; Malvolio exemplifies, Sonnet-like, the servant's fantasy of social elevation through erotic conquest; Antonio's homoerotic affection for Sebastian restates in a different key courtly devotion to the beloved as a form of service; finally, even Sir Toby follows the pattern of reciprocal service when he marries his niece's lady-in-waiting 'in recompence' for her gulling of Malvolio. (Schalkwyk 2005, p. 87)

Schalkwyk's scholarship is a laudable example of how careful historical contextualization can produce new ways of reading familiar texts. There is a method to help us to think about the importance of status in Shakespeare's stage-play worlds. Take an ordinary pack of cards and randomly distribute them in your seminar. Tell everybody that their status for the remainder of the seminar is decided by whatever card they are dealt, with Kings and Queens highest and Ace, two and three the lowest. Encourage people to move about the room revealing their cards as they wish. The point is quickly and succinctly made and it is interesting how quickly people start behaving differently according to their randomly generated status. The status card game is a practical method of bringing questions of rank and status into seminar practice, a bit of fun to make a serious point about characters in relation on stage, audiences in the theatre and wider Elizabethan society. A point is made through this exercise of more general application: societies have ideas of status, revealed or concealed, operating within them. The link for readers of *Twelfth Night* can be made to all the characters. Malvolio is perhaps a Ten who wants to be a King. Olivia and Orsino are Queen and King, the highest-status characters in the play, but they both fall for the wild-card Jack of Viola, neither male nor female. Maria is say a Seven, ranked below Malvolio, but she becomes Mistress of the Revels and in the carnival atmosphere is temporarily elevated to Queen for a day (imitating Olivia directly through her character (handwriting)). Sir Toby and Sir Andrew are knaves (Jacks) while Feste is the Joker in the pack, the true wild card: though of low status in this world (an Ace, he begs for everything) he can achieve parity with anyone through his wit. Fabian is perhaps a Five.

This may just seem like a rather petty (and simplifying) game, but it highlights issues of class and status in the play that are crucial. It helps us to become aware of how ideology might be at work in the play. On the matter of time and fortune in the play it is fascinating to note, for example, how the play 'develops a fundamental distinction between Malvolio's trust in fortune and Viola's' (Krieger 1979, p. 125). Krieger observes that Viola refers to 'this external, controlling force "time"', whereas Malvolio 'assigns all power over earthly success or failure to "fortune"' (p. 125). Viola does famously surrender to time's processes at the end of Act 2 Scene 2 when she says 'O time, thou must untangle this, not I. / It is too hard a knot for me t'untie' (2.2.40–1). Malvolio, on finding and reading the letter he believes to be from Olivia, says: ''Tis but fortune, all is fortune' (2.5.21). Malvolio's attitude is not too dissimilar to Viola's; in fact he is 'more active and more optimistic in pursuit of his fate because he has been given good reason to be so, not because he has the "wrong" attitude toward fortune' (Krieger 1979, p. 127). Malvolio is adopting the ruling-class ideology as his own by 'attributing his success, or his chances for success, to fortune, to Jove and his stars' (ibid., p. 129). The play does present us with a challenge to this ideology of fate or fortune in the figures of Feste and Maria who, 'acting upon Malvolio, represent the antithesis of chance – human will. By manipulating Malvolio, creating his destiny, they demonstrate the implicit limitation of the ruling-class attitude that "all is fortune"' (ibid., p. 129).

FURTHER RESEARCH

Students need to have good editions of the plays such as those recommended here (see the Guide to Further Reading and the Bibliography at the end of this book), and use the notes and extra material provided in introductions and appendices. They must carry out their own research. Amazingly, even now, there are unsolved Shakespearean mysteries and opportunities for new interpretations to be put forward, for new insights to be reached, by new scholars. For students of Shakespeare there will always be the thrills and excitements of scholarly detective work. The enthusiastic study of the play-texts and their contexts will be rewarded by an enhanced understanding and appreciation of Shakespeare's incredible achievement. By reading early-modern texts (books, poems, pamphlets, letters), more and more of which are available on the internet with no worrying copyright issues, we can build a sense of Shakespeare's world. All sorts of helpful search engines can help us with concordance work, enabling us to pursue key words and phrases throughout Shakespeare's work. An example will serve as a demonstration. If you key 'character' into a Shakespeare concordance search engine you come up with some interesting results: we see Shakespeare discovering the modern use of the term, perhaps developing it rather than discovering it. In *Hamlet*, for example, we find Claudius reading a letter from Hamlet:

> 'Tis Hamlet's character. 'Naked!'
> And in a postscript here, he says 'alone.'
> Can you advise me? (*Hamlet* 4.7.49–51)

Hamlet, alone and naked, reveals his character to King Claudius and to all who try to read his characters, the impressions he makes on this world. In *Measure for Measure* we find the mysterious Duke Vincentio addressing his deputy Angelo: 'Angelo, / There is a kind of character in thy life, / That to the observer doth thy history / Fully unfold' (*Measure for Measure* 1.1.33–6). It is the readers and watchers of the play who are the observers to whom the life of characters can fully unfold.

The ambition of the author of this little book is to make the reader hungry, to encourage an appetite for more and more information and context. Educating ourselves is rewarded by some satisfying and enriching discoveries that add depth to our engagement with texts – and Shakespeare's texts reward this hungry critical approach as much, and more, than any other. For not only are the texts, including *Twelfth Night*, themselves so rich, but there is a huge critical and performance history available to us in which jewels of insight and understanding glimmer. There is, too, we must be confident, plenty more to come.

So this ends rather unfashionably, arguing that *Twelfth Night* is a play about Shakespeare's characters in love, with each other, with themselves, with food and drink, with music and song, with wit and fooling, with transgression and revelry, with language itself. It is a play about characters in love with life, and with youth, which will not endure.

Twelfth Night is about the transitory nature of youth and beauty. We are reminded in one of Feste's songs that, though we may be enjoying the comedy we watch ('present mirth hath present laughter'), there will come a time when we will not be as fresh-faced and ready to answer the call of love: 'Youth's a stuff will not endure' (2.3.46, 50). The reflection is instigated by the question 'What is love?' (2.3.45) and the thought that, as Edmund Spenser so beautifully phrased it in 'February' of *The Shepheardes Calender* (1579), 'All that is lent to love, wyll be lost' (Spenser 1993, p. 512). Such a sense of time's inevitable passage and the decay and demise of everything haunts the play with a melancholy that can never quite be forgotten, certainly not by Feste. The lovers at the end of the play, under Orsino's instruction, await the moment that 'golden time convents' (5.1.372) ('convents' here is variously interpreted as 'comes about' (Oxford) or 'summons' (Arden) or 'calls' (Cambridge)). This is an optimistic and hopeful notion of the future, a direct tonic to Feste's preceding and dispiriting 'and thus the whirligig of time brings in his revenges' (5.1.366–7), or the rather wistful song he ends the play with. Orsino's vision of 'golden time' echoes another use by Shakespeare in his Sonnets (in which the fundamental fact of time passing and life moving ever toward death is omnipresent):

> Thou art thy mother's glass, and she in thee
> Calls back the lovely April of her prime;
> So thou through windows of thine age shalt see,
> Despite of wrinkles, this thy golden time.

But if thou live remembered not to be
Die single, and thine images die with thee. (Sonnet 3)

Twelfth Night ends in marriages between, we imagine, fertile young couples whose passion for each other surely promises a future generation of healthy children. And in Feste's final song the link is made to another golden time, the time of all our childhoods, in the opening line: 'When that I was but a little tiny boy'.

GUIDE TO FURTHER READING

This is a selective, annotated list that gives students a guide to the editions of the play and secondary texts most useful as a starting point for further research.

Barber, C. L. (1959), *Shakespeare's Festive Comedy*. Princeton: Princeton University Press. Barber's investigation into English festival traditions and their relation to Shakespeare's comedy provides a helpful starting point for the modern scholar.

Billington, Michael (ed.), with Bill Alexander, John Barton, John Caird and Terry Hands (1990), *Directors' Shakespeare: Approaches to 'Twelfth Night'*. London: Nick Hern. This is a wide-ranging discussion between directors of the play which makes for a fascinating read. Full of insights into questions that have to be addressed in rehearsal and performance.

Donno, Elizabeth Story (ed.) (1985), *Twelfth Night*. Cambridge Shakespeare 3. Cambridge: Cambridge University Press. This edition has an illustrated introduction, sets out the play-text clearly and provides some helpful and informative notes.

Draper, John W. (1950), *The Twelfth Night of Shakespeare's Audience*. Stanford, CA: Stanford University Press. Draper's character-based approach to the play grounds its argument on historical contextualization. A contagious enthusiasm for the play is evident throughout.

Edmondson, Paul (2005), *The Shakespeare Handbooks: Twelfth Night*. Basingstoke: Palgrave Macmillan. Edmondson offers commentary, contextual documents, a sampling of critical responses and some case studies of key performances. A useful and worthwhile volume for the student of *Twelfth Night*.

Ford, John R. (2006), *Twelfth Night: A Guide to the Play*. Westport, CT: Greenwood Press. Ford has produced a remarkably concentrated guide to the play which covers textual history, contexts and sources, dramatic structure, themes and critical approaches. There is a particularly strong strand of performance criticism in this volume.

Hotson, Leslie (1954), *The First Night of 'Twelfth Night'*. London: Rupert Hart-Davis. An amazing, if quirky, attempt to prove his thesis that *Twelfth Night* was commissioned for the state visit of Don Virginio Orsino and was first performed in the Great Hall of Whitehall Palace. Hotson's volume is a mine of intriguing contextual information.

Lothian, J. M. and Craik, T. W. (1975), *Twelfth Night*. The Arden Shakespeare. London: Routledge. A detailed introduction and good notes make this a suitable edition for students of the play.

Mahood, M. M. (ed.) (1968), *Twelfth Night*. New Penguin Shakespeare. London: Penguin. Revised edition published in 2005 with a new introduction by Michael Dobson. Good reading edition of the play-text.

McDonald, Russ (2004), *Shakespeare: An Anthology of Criticism and Theory 1945–2000*. London: Blackwell. This is an extremely useful compendium of important criticism from the last few decades. All students of Shakespeare will find stimulating content here.

Warren, Roger and Wells, Stanley (eds) (1994), *Twelfth Night*. Oxford Shakespeare. Oxford: Oxford University Press. This is a very full edition with an excellent introduction, extensive notes, and songs with music printed as an appendix (edited by musician and composer James Walker). This edition has been used as the source for all quotations from the play given in this book.

BIBLIOGRAPHY

PRIMARY

The following is a list of all the primary texts quoted from or referred to in the previous chapters.

Bate, Jonathan and Rasmussen, Eric (2007), *William Shakespeare: Complete Works*. Basingstoke: Macmillan.

Donno, Elizabeth Story (ed.) (1985), *Twelfth Night*. Cambridge Shakespeare 3. Cambridge: Cambridge University Press.

Kerrigan, John (1999), *Shakespeare's Sonnets*. London: Penguin.

Latham, Agnes (ed.) (1975), *As You Like It*. Arden Shakespeare. London: Thomson.

Lothian, J. M. and Craik, T. W. (1975), *Twelfth Night*. The Arden Shakespeare. London: Routledge.

Mahood, M. M. (ed.) (1968; revised edn 2005), *Twelfth Night*. New Penguin Shakespeare. London: Penguin.

Thompson, Ann and Taylor, Neil (eds) (2006), *Hamlet*. Arden Shakespeare. London: Thomson.

Warren, Roger and Wells, Stanley (eds) (1994), *Twelfth Night*. Oxford Shakespeare. Oxford: Oxford University Press.

Secondary

The following is a list of all the secondary texts quoted from or referred to in the previous chapters.

Ackroyd, Peter (2005), *Shakespeare: The Biography*. London: Chatto and Windus.

Adland, David (1973), *The Group Approach to Shakespeare: Twelfth Night*. London: Longman.

Aristotle, Horace, Longinus (trans. T. S. Dorsch) (1965), *Classical Literary Criticism*. London: Penguin.

Armstrong, Katherine and Atkin, Graham (1998), *Studying Shakespeare: A Practical Guide*. London: Prentice Hall.

Atkin, Graham, Walsh, Chris and Watkins, Susan (eds) (1995), *Studying Literature: A Practical Introduction*. London: Harvester Wheatsheaf.

Barber, C. L. (1959), *Shakespeare's Festive Comedy*. Princeton: Princeton University Press.

Barton, John (1984), *Playing Shakespeare*. London: Methuen.

Bassnett, Susan (1993), *Shakespeare: The Elizabethan Plays*. Basingstoke: Macmillan.

Bevington, David (2002), *Shakespeare*. London: Blackwell.

Billington, Michael (ed.), with Bill Alexander, John Barton, John Caird and Terry Hands (1990), *Directors' Shakespeare: Approaches to 'Twelfth Night'*. London: Nick Hern.

Bloom, Harold (ed.) (1987), *William Shakespeare's 'Twelfth Night'*. Modern Critical Interpretations. New York: Chelsea House Publications.

Bradley, A. C. (1985), *Shakespearean Tragedy* (revised edition). London: Macmillan.

Byrne, M. St Clare (1961), *Elizabethan Life in Town and Country*. London: Methuen.

Champion, Larry S. (1970), *The Evolution of Shakespeare's Comedy*. Cambridge, MA: Harvard University Press.

Draper, John W. (1950), *The Twelfth Night of Shakespeare's Audience*. Stanford, CA: Stanford University Press.

Edmondson, Paul (2005), *The Shakespeare Handbooks: Twelfth Night*. Basingstoke: Palgrave Macmillan.

Evans, G. Blakemore (1987), *Elizabethan–Jacobean Drama*. London: A & C Black.

Fielding, Emma (2002), *Twelfth Night*. Actors on Shakespeare. London: Faber and Faber.

Ford, John R. (2006), *Twelfth Night: A Guide to the Play*. Westport, CT: Greenwood Press.

Frye, Northrop (1965), *A Natural Perspective: The Development of Shakespearean Comedy and Romance*. London: Columbia University Press.

Gay, Penny (1994), *As She Likes It: Shakespeare's Unruly Women*. London: Routledge.

Goldsmith, Robert Hillis (1974), *Wise Fools in Shakespeare*. Liverpool: Liverpool University Press.

Greenblatt, Stephen (1988), *Shakespearean Negotiations: The Circulation of Social Energy in Renaissance England*. Oxford: Clarendon Press.

Grimal, Pierre (1986), *The Dictionary of Classical Mythology*. Oxford: Blackwell.

Gurr, Andrew (1980), *The Shakespearean Stage, 1574–1642*. London: Cambridge University Press.

Halliday, F. E. (1964), *A Shakespeare Companion*. London, Penguin.

Hotson, Leslie (1954), *The First Night of 'Twelfth Night'*. London: Rupert Hart-Davis.

Howard, Jean (1988), 'Crossdressing, the theatre, and gender struggle in early modern England', *Shakespeare Quarterly*, 39.

Jardine, Lisa (1989), *Still Harping on Daughters: Women and Drama in the Age of Shakespeare*. Hemel Hempstead: Harvester Wheatsheaf.

Krieger, Elliot (1979), *A Marxist Study of Shakespeare's Comedies*. London: Macmillan.

McDonald, Russ (2004), *Shakespeare: An Anthology of Criticism and Theory 1945–2000*. London: Blackwell.

McLeish, Kenneth (1985), *Longman Guide to Shakespeare's Characters*. London: Longman.

Maguire, Laurie E. (2004), *Studying Shakespeare: A Guide to the Plays*. London: Blackwell.

Montaigne, Michel de (trans. M. A. Screech) (1987), *The Complete Essays*. London: Penguin.

Noble, Richmond (1935), *Shakespeare's Biblical Knowledge and Use of the Book of Common Prayer*. London: Macmillan.

Nunn, Trevor (1996), *William Shakespeare's Twelfth Night: A Screenplay*. London: Methuen Drama.

Onions, C. T. (1958), *A Shakespeare Glossary*. London: Oxford University Press.

Palmer, D. J. (ed.) (1972), *Shakespeare: Twelfth Night*. Casebook Series. Basingstoke: Macmillan.

Pennington, Michael (2000), *Twelfth Night: A User's Guide*. London: Nick Hern.

Potter, Lois (1985), *Twelfth Night: Text and Performance*. Basingstoke: Macmillan.

Rivkin, Julie and Ryan, Michael (eds) (1998), *Literary Theory: An Anthology*. Oxford: Blackwell.

Salgado, Gamini (ed.) (1972), *Cony-Catchers and Bawdy-Baskets: An Anthology of Elizabethan Low Life*. London: Penguin.

Schalkwyk, David (2005) 'Love and service in *Twelfth Night* and the Sonnets', *Shakespeare Quarterly*, 56.

Schoenbaum, S. (1975), *William Shakespeare: A Documentary Life*. Oxford: Clarendon Press.

Selden, Raman (ed.) (1988), *The Theory of Criticism: From Plato to the Present, A Reader*. London: Longman.

Smith, Emma (ed.) (2004), *Shakespeare's Comedies*. Oxford: Blackwell.

Spenser, Edmund (Hugh Maclean and Anne Lake Prescott, eds) (1993), *Edmund Spenser's Poetry*. A Norton Critical Edition (third edition). New York: Norton.

Styan, J. L. (1965), *The Dramatic Experience*. Cambridge: Cambridge University Press.

Tillyard, E. M. W. (1943), *The Elizabethan World Picture*. Harmondsworth: Penguin.

Waller, Gary (ed.) (1991), *Shakespeare's Comedies*. London: Longman.

Wayne, Valerie (ed.) (1991), *The Matter of Difference*. Hemel Hempstead: Harvester.

White, R. S. (ed.) (1996), *New Casebooks: Twelfth Night*. Basingstoke: Macmillan.

INDEX